TABLE OF CONTENTS

PREFACE

This report assesses the activities of organized crime groups, terrorist groups, and narcotics traffickers in general in the Tri-Border Area (TBA) of Argentina, Brazil, and Paraguay, focusing mainly on the period since 1999. Some of the related topics discussed, such as governmental and police corruption and anti–money-laundering laws, may also apply in part to the three TBA countries in general in addition to the TBA. This is unavoidable because the TBA cannot be discussed entirely as an isolated entity.

Based entirely on open sources, this assessment has made extensive use of books, journal articles, and other reports available in the Library of Congress collections. It is based in part on the author's earlier research paper entitled "Narcotics-Funded Terrorist/Extremist Groups in Latin America" (May 2002). It has also made extensive use of sources available on the Internet, including Argentine, Brazilian, and Paraguayan newspaper articles. One of the most relevant Spanish-language sources used for this assessment was Mariano César Bartolomé's paper entitled *Amenazas a la seguridad de los estados: La triple frontera como 'área gris' en el cono sur americano* [Threats to the Security of States: The Triborder as a 'Grey Area' in the Southern Cone of South America] (2001). The selective bibliography includes books, journal articles, and other reports. Newspaper and magazine articles are footnoted. This report also includes an appendix containing brief profiles of five alleged operatives of Islamic fundamentalist groups in the TBA and a diagram of drug-trafficking routes in the region.

The information cutoff date used in this report is July 2003. Thus, it lacks any updated information about the individuals discussed in it. However, the study has been partially edited as of November 2010 to reflect the fact that Rajkumar Sabnani or Rajkumar Naraindas Sabnani, whose alleged fund-raising or money laundering on behalf of TBA extremists was reported in the original edition, has been completely exonerated of any involvement. Sabnani is a prominent and respected businessman residing in Hong Kong. Moreover, criminal proceedings against Sabnani's relatives and employees in Paraguay were officially closed, and all parties were acquitted and absolved of any guilt or punishment in July 2007. Therefore, the information about Sabnani and his associates has been removed from this version of the study.

EXECUTIVE SUMMARY

Islamic Terrorist Groups and Activities in the Tri-Border Area (TBA)

This review of the available open-source information on Islamic terrorist group activities in Tri-Border Area (TBA) during the 1999 to 2003 period provides substantial evidence for concluding that various Islamic terrorist groups have used the TBA—where Argentina, Brazil, and Paraguay meet—as a haven for fund-raising, recruiting, plotting terrorist attacks elsewhere in the TBA countries or the Americas in general, and other such activities. Islamic terrorist groups with a presence in the TBA reportedly include Egypt's Al-Gama'a al-Islamiyya (Islamic Group) and Al-Jihad (Islamic Jihad), al Qaeda, Hamas, Hizballah, and al-Muqawamah (the Resistance; also spelled al-Moqawama), which is a pro-Iran wing of the Lebanon-based Hizballah. Islamic terrorist groups have used the TBA for fund-raising, drug trafficking, money laundering, plotting, and other activities in support of their organizations. The large Arab community in the TBA is highly conducive to the establishment of sleeper cells of Islamic terrorists, including Hizballah and al Qaeda. Nevertheless, as many as 11,000 members of the Islamic community in the TBA may have moved since late 2001 to other less closely watched Arab population centers in South America.

Hizballah clearly derives a quite substantial amount of income from its various illicit activities in the TBA, in addition to financial support from the government of Iran and income derived from narcotics trafficking in Lebanon's Al Beqa'a Valley. Reports of Iranian intelligence agents being implicated in Hizballah-linked activities in the TBA since the early 1990s suggest direct Iranian government support of Hizballah activities in the region. Lebanese government political support of the sizeable Lebanese community in the TBA extends to Hizballah members in the region because of Hizballah's influence in Lebanon's politics and society.

News media reports in recent years of al Qaeda's presence in the TBA and of cooperation between Hizballah and al Qaeda in the region first surfaced in mid-1999, based on reported identification of al Qaeda operatives in the TBA by Argentine intelligence. The conventional thinking is that the Sunni-oriented al Qaeda and the Shi'ite-oriented Hizballah would never cooperate, but it seems more likely that the reported cooperation is emblematic of a larger strategic alliance between the two organizations.[1] News media reports since 1999 of foiled terrorist plots against U.S. embassies and the arrest of several terrorists linked to al Qaeda—including Ali Khalil Mehri, El Said Hassan Ali Mohammed Mukhlis, Marwan 'Adnan al-Qadi ("Marwan al-Safadi"), and Mohamed Ali Aboul-Ezz Al-Mahdi Ibrahim Soliman (also spelled Mohamad Ali Abao-Ezz El-Mahdi Ibrahim Suliman)—suggest that al Qaeda has a presence in the region. Al Qaeda may have begun to establish a network in the TBA when Osama bin Laden and Khalid Sheikh Mohammed reportedly visited the area in 1995. Al Qaeda's activities in the TBA are reportedly linked to trafficking of arms, drugs, and uranium, as well as money laundering, in association with Chinese and Russian (Chechen) mafias.

If a Cable News Network (CNN) report is correct that an Islamic terrorist summit was held in the TBA in late 2002 to plan terrorist attacks against U.S. and Israeli diplomatic facilities in the South American region, then attacking these targets would appear to be a high priority for al Qaeda, Hizballah, and other Islamic terrorist groups that may have a presence in the TBA. Plotting by TBA-based terrorists linked to Hizballah and al Qaeda to blow up the U.S. Embassy in Asunción began in 1996. The embassy most likely remains one of the primary U.S. targets of Islamic terrorist groups in the region. In 2000-01, TBA-based al Qaeda operatives expanded their targeting to include the U.S. and Israeli embassies in Asunción and the U.S. embassies in Montevideo and Quito (Israel closed its embassy in Asunción in early 2002). The pattern of these foiled plots strongly suggests that TBA-based Hizballah and/or al Qaeda operatives will again attempt to carry out simultaneous terrorist attacks against two or more U.S. embassies or consulates in South America. Targets could also include hotels, tourism centers, airports, or multinational companies, especially those of Israeli, German, French, or U.S. origin.[2]

Organized Crime Groups and Activities in the TBA

In addition to Islamic terrorist groups, the TBA provides a haven that is geographically, socially, economically, and politically highly conducive for allowing organized crime and the

---

[1] Hisham al-Qarawi, "Has Bin-Ladin Made An Alliance With Mughanniyah in Latin America?" *Al-Arab al-Alamiyah* [London-based Libyan daily providing independent coverage of Arab and international issues with a strong pro-Libyan, Arab nationalist, and anti-United States editorial line], November 14, 2002, 2, as translated from the Arabic for FBIS, "Article Views Possibility of Al-Qa'ida-Hizballah Alliance in Latin America," November 14, 2002 (FBIS Document ID: GMP20021114000092).

[2] María Luisa Mac Kay, *Clarín* staff, *Clarín* (Internet version-www), October 18, 2002, as translated by FBIS Document ID: LAP20021018000021, "Argentina Put on Heightened Security Alert in View of Potential Terrorist Attack," October 18, 2002.

corrupt officials who accept their bribes or payoffs to operate in a symbiotic relationship that thrives on drug and arms trafficking, money laundering, and other lucrative criminal activities. As of 2001, money laundering in the TBA, aided by special CC-5 accounts for non-residents and other mechanisms, reportedly was averaging US$12 billion a year. Ciudad del Este and Foz do Iguaçu are the region's principal money-laundering centers. Ciudad del Este was generating US$12 to US$13 billion in cash transactions annually, making it the third city worldwide behind Hong Kong and Miami. However, that figure may have fallen since then as a result of stricter Argentine and Brazilian customs systems.

Numerous organized crime groups, including the Lebanese Mafia, are known to use the TBA for illicit activities such as smuggling, money laundering, and product piracy. Although it is unclear whether the Lebanese Mafia and Hizballah are basically synonymous or entirely separate entities, there is probably a close relationship between them. In any case, the Hizballah organization in the TBA is known to collaborate with various mafias, including the Hong Kong Mafia.

Indigenous crime groups operating in the TBA include the Argentine, Brazilian, and Paraguayan mafias. Non-indigenous mafias operating in the TBA reportedly include syndicates from Chile, China, Colombia, Corsica, Ghana, Libya, Italy, Ivory Coast, Japan, Korea, Lebanon, Nigeria, Russia, and Taiwan. However, a review of open-source news media found information indicating activities mainly by the Chinese, Korean, Lebanese, and Taiwanese mafias. The thriving business of importing counterfeit Compact Disks (CDs) and CD-ROMs from Asia is linked to organized crime in Korea, Lebanon, Libya, and Taiwan. The Hong Kong Mafia is particularly active in large-scale trafficking of pirated products from mainland China to Ciudad del Este and maintains strong ties with Hizballah in the TBA. Unspecified Chinese mafias in the TBA are reportedly seeking to expand into Argentina in order to establish themselves into the duty-free zone of San Luis Province. At least two Chinese mafia groups in the TBA—the Sung-I and Ming families—engage in illegal operations with the Egyptian al-Gama'a al-Islamiyya (Islamic Group).

Efforts to Counter the Use of the TBA by Organized Crime and Terrorist Groups

Cooperative and individual national efforts of the Argentine, Brazilian, and Paraguayan security forces to fight illicit activities by organized crime and terrorist groups in the TBA appear to have constrained these activities since late 2001, but by no means eliminated them. Their efforts have been hindered by endemic corruption within the police, criminal justice systems, and governments of the TBA countries; poor pay; inadequate training, equipment, funding, law-enforcement techniques, and penal codes; poor organization; human rights abuses; weak anti-money-laundering laws and enforcement thereof; and secrecy provisions of banking laws (with the exception of Paraguay, whose problem has more to do with not reporting suspicious financial activities).

INTRODUCTION

Several free-trade Latin American areas with large Middle Eastern populations allow Islamic terrorist groups, organized crime mafias, and corrupt officials to thrive in a mutually beneficial, symbiotic relationship. These areas include Colombia's Maicao, Venezuela's Margarita Island, Chile's Iquique, and the Tri-Border Area (TBA). This study focuses on the largest and most significant of these areas—the TBA, an enclave adjoining Argentina, Brazil, and Paraguay.

Estimates of how much organized crime and corrupt officials profit from these duty-free zones are unavailable, but it is estimated that Islamic fundamentalist groups in the TBA and similar areas in Latin America are sending between US$300 million and US$500 million a year in profits from drug trafficking, arms dealing, and other illegal activities, including money laundering, contraband, and product piracy, to radical Islamic groups in the Middle East.[3] The TBA's Islamic extremist support networks include, in addition to Margarita Island and Iquique, various other centers of Arab population in the region, such as the Paraguayan city of Encarnación, on the border with Argentina, and the Uruguayan town of Chuy, on the border with Brazil.

---

[3] "U.S. General: Islamic Rebels Get Cash from Latin America Gangs," *Orlando Sentinel*, March 10, 2003, A9, citing General James T. Hill, commander of the U.S. Southern Command in Miami.

Hizballah clerics and members of other violent Islamic groups reportedly began planting agents and recruiting sympathizers among Arab and Muslim immigrants in Latin America in the mid-1980s, at the height of the Lebanese civil war. Hizballah cells began to form in the TBA as a result of Hizballah proselytizing in the Lebanese communities. Islamic fundamentalist organizations such as the Islamic Resistance Movement (Harakat al-Muqawamah al-Islamiyya—Hamas), Hizballah, and al-Gama'a al-Islamiyya (Islamic Group) actively use the TBA as a support base, and al Qaeda reportedly has been establishing a presence in the region since at least the mid-1990s. By mid-2000, an estimated 460 Hizballah operatives were thought to be living and working in the TBA.[4] Numerous Lebanese and Palestinian extremists arrived in the TBA from Colombia in October 2000.[5]

With the help of organized crime and corrupt officials, these Islamic terrorist organizations use the TBA to raise revenues through illicit activities that include drug- and arms-trafficking, counterfeiting, money laundering, forging travel documents, and even pirating software and music. In addition, they provide haven and assistance to other terrorists transiting the region. Al Qaeda reportedly also does considerable fund-raising in Ciudad del Este.[6]

Suspected Hizballah terrorists have also used the TBA as a base for carrying out two major terrorist attacks in Buenos Aires in the early 1990s—one against the Israeli Embassy on March 17, 1992; and the other against a Jewish community center on July 18, 1994. Since the 1994 attack, Islamic terrorists in the TBA have largely confined their activities to criminal fund-raising and other activities in support of their terrorist organizations, including plotting terrorist actions to be carried out in other countries.

This study has confirmed the likely close interrelation among Islamic terrorist fund-raising and money-laundering activities, organized crime, and corruption of public officials in the TBA. All of the TBA's terrorist and organized crime activities are facilitated by official corruption, which, in turn, is fueled by the profits of lucrative criminal activities, which are

---

[4] Harris Whitbeck and Ingrid Arneson, "Terrorists Find Haven in South America," CNN.com, November 8, 2001, http://www.cnn.com/2001/WORLD/americas/11/07/inv.terror.south.

[5] Their names, as published in the Paraguayan press, included: Abadia Abu Sakran, Ayman Taha, Baha El-Khatis, Samer Sweileh, Diban Abu Gamous, Asan Hamaida, Mohamed Minirouwi, Hamad Hamad, Ayman Abu Yin, Salah Tinme, Wael Nasser, Sharif Tahayna, Abbas Ouweiwi, Nasser Saha Ane, Muhammad Moussa Hassan Gadalah, Rafat Rahdan Salem Abio, Brahim Un-Karim Bani-Uda, Mahmud Zakar Rages Zatma Adnan, and Mahimud Jabber Alul. Bartolomé, 11, citing "Antiterroristas remiten las evidencias al fiscal" [Antiterrorists provide the judge with evidence], *Noticias*, December 5, 2000.

[6] Jeffrey Goldberg, "In the Party of God," *The New Yorker* 79, no. 32 (October 28, 2002).

conducted like business enterprises by organized crime and terrorist groups. In effect, a mutually beneficial nexus exists among these three sectors. The TBA serves as a microcosm for examining this relationship.

GEOGRAPHY, SOCIETY, AND ECONOMY

Geography

The TBA's porous borders are defined by three closely grouped population centers, one in each of three countries: the Argentine city of Puerto Iguazú, the Brazilian city of Foz do Iguaçu, and the Paraguayan city of Ciudad del Este (formerly Puerto Presidente Stroessner). The region's most famous landmark is Iguassú Falls (Port., Iguaçu Falls), which straddles the Argentina-Brazil border in Brazil's Paraná State and Argentina's Misiones Province.

In the early 1970s, when Brazil and Paraguay were seeking to exploit the energy-generating and tourist potential of Iguassú Falls and to promote regional trade, government planners established a free-trade zone in the rapidly growing boomtown city of Ciudad del Este, thereby allowing Argentines and Brazilians to purchase cheap electronic products there.[7] The TBA, with already more than half a million inhabitants, soon became a lawless jungle corner of Argentina, Brazil, and Paraguay.

Ciudad del Este

Ciudad del Este, located 330 kilometers to the east of Asunción, is the capital of Paraguay's Upper Paraná Department and the country's second-largest city. In 2003 Ciudad del Este had an estimated population of 239,500.[8] Strategically located, Ciudad del Este is situated

---

[7] Sebastian Junger, "Terrorism's New Geography," *Vanity Fair*, no. 508 (December 2002), 196, citing Brazilian journalist Jackson Lima.
[8] Stefan Helders, "Paraguay," *The World Gazetteer*, 2003, http://www.world-gazetteer.com/c/c_py.htm#pl_37.

on the Pan American Highway, which runs from Asunción, Paraguay, to Curitiba, Brazil, located near the port of Paranaguá.

Foz do Iguaçu

The Brazilian city of Foz do Iguaçu (formerly spelled Foz do Iguassú), Paraná State, has been recently described in news media as having a population of about 300,000. (According to the 1996 census, its population was 231,627.[9]) Many people leave Ciudad del Este at night and cross the 303-meter-long, concrete bridge, the Friendship International Bridge (Sp., Puente Internacional de la Amistad; or Port., Ponte Internacional da Amizade), to return to Foz do Iguaçu, where the quality of life is better than in Ciudad del Este. Nevertheless, violent crime is a serious problem in Foz do Iguaçu, where 180 homicides were reported in 2000, 243 in 2001, and 275 in 2002.[10] (By comparison, the number of homicides in the top-ranking U.S. city in 2002, Washington, D.C., with about 2 ½ times the population, was 262.)

Puerto Iguazú

Argentina's Puerto Iguazú, with a population of approximately 29,000, is located at the confluence of the Paraná and Iguazú (Port., Iguassú) rivers in the northwest corner of Misiones

---

[9] Demographia: Brasil [Brazil]: Cities (Municipalities) Over 100,000 Population: 1996, http://www.demographia.com/db-brasil-city96.htm.

[10] "Homicide Rate Declines in Foz do Iguaçu," *A Gazeta do Iguaçu* [Foz do Iguaçu; independent, largest-circulation daily in the TBA; offers balanced reporting and daily editorial comment], citing data released by the Legal Medical Institute (IML), as translated by FBIS Document ID: LAP20030606000016, June 5, 2003.

Province. The Atlantic Ocean can be accessed from Puerto Iguazú using small freighters. Although Puerto Iguazú is isolated from Ciudad del Este by the Paraná, Puerto Iguazú has access to Brazil's Foz do Iguaçu across the Iguazú at the 489-meter-long Tancredo Neves International Bridge. The Arab immigrants of Foz do Iguaçu and Ciudad del Este generally avoid visiting Puerto Iguazú because they reportedly do not feel welcome there and are regarded suspiciously by Argentine security officials.[11]

Society

The General Population of the TBA

By 2001, the TBA had a highly heterogeneous population of more than 700,000, including the area outside the three cities.[12] Foz do Iguaçu's population includes an estimated 65 different nationalities.[13]

The three main ethnic communities in Ciudad del Este are the Chinese, Lebanese, and Korean.[14] In 2001, the city's largest ethnic group was the Chinese, with about 30,000 members, of whom only about 9,000 may be registered legally.[15] The Portuguese language predominates. Guaraní is generally spoken by the city's poor Paraguayan residents. Arabic is heard as much as, or perhaps more than, Spanish. Chinese and Korean are also commonly heard.[16] Ciudad del Este's Chinese residents, mostly from China's southern Canton region, prefer this city over Foz do Iguaçu.

---

[11] Franco Iacomini, "Fronteira sem lei: A divisa com o Paraguai é a dor de cabeça do Mercosul" [Lawless Border: The Division with Paraguay and Mercosul's Headache], *Veja* [São Paulo], no. 1541 (April 8, 1998), http://veja.abril.uol.com.br/080498/p_044.html.

[12] Mariano César Bartolomé, *Amenzas a la seguridad de los estados: La triple frontera como 'área gris' en el cono sur americano* [Threats to the Security of States: The Triborder Region as a 'Grey Area' in the American Southern Cone]. Buenos Aires, November 29, 2001, http://www.geocities.com/mcbartolome/triplefrontera1.htm; reprinted as Dr. Mariano César Bartolomé, "La triple frontera: Principal foco de inseguridad en el Cono Sur Americano" [The triborder: Principal focus of insecurity in the American southern cone], *Military Review*, July–August 2002 (Spanish edition), http://www-cgsc.army.mil/milrev/spanish/JulAug02/indxjasp.asp.

[13] Bartolomé, 3, citing a 2001 estimate by Brazil's Federal Police (Polícia Federal—PF).

[14] Ricardo Grinbaum, "In Paraguay, Smugglers' Paradise," *World Press Review*, 43, no.1 (January 1996): 25–26 (reprinted from *Veja*).

[15] Bartolomé, 7.

[16] Franco Iacomini, "Fronteira sem lei: A divisa com o Paraguai é a dor de cabeça do Mercosul" [Lawless Border: The Division with Paraguay and Mercosul's Headache], *Veja* [São Paulo], no. 1541 (April 8, 1998), http://veja.abril.uol.com.br/080498/p_044.html.

Muslim Population

The TBA has one of the most important Arab communities in South America. Of the Arab population in Ciudad del Este and Foz do Iguaçu, an estimated 90 percent is of Lebanese origin.[17] Estimates of the size of the Arab community of immigrants in the TBA (mainly in Ciudad del Este and Foz do Iguaçu) range from 20,000 to 30,000, with most residing in Foz do Iguaçu.[18] Of these general figures, Foz do Iguaçu's Arab population accounts for 10,000 to 21,000 Arabs of Palestinian and Lebanese descent.[19]

The Arab community in the TBA is tightly knit, with its own schools and clubs, making outside penetration very difficult. Most Arab immigrants in Foz do Iguaçu live in gated condominiums.[20] The cultural and social demographics of Ciudad del Este and Foz do Iguaçu make an ideal operations base for Arabic-speaking terrorist or criminal groups. A few extremists can get together, form a highly secure cell, carry out their mission, and return with alibis backed up by many in the community. Sympathizers of al Qaeda have allegedly been active in the TBA for these reasons.

---

[17] Bartolomé, 4.

[18] The *New York Times* reports that "more than 20,000 Middle Eastern immigrants, most from Lebanon and Syria, live in the area." See Larry Rohter, "South America Region Under Watch for Signs of Terrorists," *New York Times*, December 15, 2002, 1A, 32. *Jane's* notes that the region's 629,000 population includes 23,000 Arabs of Palestinian and Lebanese descent. See John Daly, "The Suspects: The Latin American Connection," *Jane's Terrorism & Security Monitor*, October 1, 2001. The 30,000 figure is cited by Marc Perelman, *U.S. Joining Terrorism Probe Along Lawless Brazil Border: Hezbollah, Al Qaeda Links Sought.* The Lebanese Foundation for Peace (LFP), December 13, 2002, http://www.free-lebanon.com/LFPNews/2002/terrorprobe/terrorprobe.html.

[19] *A Gazeta do Iguaçu* [Foz do Iguaçu], "Muslims Prevail Among Small Religions in Foz," February 3, 2003, as translated for FBIS, "Highlights From the Tri-Border Press for the Week 3-7 February," February 11, 2003 (FBIS Document ID: LAP20030211000124).

[20] "Argentina, Paraguay, Brazil Step Up Search for "terrorists" in Triborder Area," BBC Monitoring Service [UK], September 15, 2001.

Argentina's total Muslim population is known to be approximately three times as large as its Jewish population. Estimates of the former range from 700,000 to 900,000, with the lower figure considered by some researchers to be more likely.[21] The number of Jews living in Argentina is estimated to be about 250,000, of whom about 80 percent live in Buenos Aires.[22] Argentina's Jewish population has been the target of terrorism by Islamic fundamentalists and neo-Nazis.

Foz do Iguaçu reportedly has Brazil's second-largest Arab community (São Paulo may have the largest).[23] Nevertheless, Foz do Iguaçu's Arab population seems relatively small in comparison with a reported 1 million Muslims who have Brazilian citizenship and live in Brazil. Most Brazilian Muslims came from Lebanon, Syria, Palestine, Egypt, and other countries, but those in Foz do Iguaçu are mostly of Lebanese and Palestinian descent. Many members of the Arab population of Foz do Iguaçu and its surrounding hinterlands maintain commercial outlets in Ciudad del Este.

Economy

Ciudad del Este is an oasis for informants and spies; peddlers of contraband (largely cheap East Asian goods) and counterfeit products; traffickers in drugs, weapons, and humans (prostitutes, including women and children forced into prostitution); common criminals; mafia organizations; and undocumented Islamic terrorists. In Ciudad del Este, street merchants sell not only cheap trinkets and counterfeit products, but also items such as an AK-47 for US$375.[24] Despite its seedy appearance, Ciudad del Este is a world-class center of commerce in terms of cash transactions. Thanks to the presence of organized crime, the city's retail economy ranked third worldwide—behind Hong Kong and Miami—in volume of cash transactions, peaking at

---

[21] Pedro Brieger and Enrique Herszkowich, "The Muslim Community of Argentina," *The Muslim World* [Hartford], 92, nos. ½ (Spring 2002): 157–68.

[22] Jacob Kovadloff, *Crisis In Argentina*. American Jewish Community [New York], circa June 2002, http://www.ajc.org/InTheMedia/PublicationsPrint.asp?did=555.

[23] *Gazeta do Iguaçu* [Foz do Iguaçu], "Muslims Prevail Among Small Religions in Foz," February 3, 2003, as translated for FBIS, "Highlights From the Tri-Border Press for the Week 3-7 February," February 11, 2003 (FBIS Document ID: LAP20030211000124); and "Palestinian Community in Brazil," *Jornal do Iguaçu* [Foz do Iguaçu], September 27, 2002, as translated for FBIS, "Highlights: Brazil - Paraguay Triborder Press 23-27 Sep 02," September 30, 2002 (FBIS Document ID: LAP20020930000045).

[24] Jeffrey Goldberg, "In the Party of God," *The New Yorker* 79, no. 32 (October 28, 2002).

US$12 billion in 1994.[25] In 2001 the estimated annual turnover in Ciudad del Este made the city's economy larger than that of the rest of Paraguay.[26] The relatively small Arab community in Ciudad del Este is among Latin America's most prosperous and influential.

The region's main economic dynamic is business between Ciudad del Este and Foz do Iguaçu. On normal days, an estimated 30,000 to 40,000 people and 20,000 vehicles cross the Friendship Bridge between Brazil and Paraguay. Residents and tourists in Ciudad del Este also regularly cross between Paraguay and Brazil on foot, often without documents. Border checks by authorities have generally been limited to simple spot-checks, and less than 10 percent of personal baggage or vehicle loads are checked. The traditional status of the TBA as a source of cheap goods has been severely restricted, however, by new regulations issued by Argentina and Brazil. After Brazil implemented an integrated customs system to combat smuggling, commerce between Ciudad del Este and Foz do Iguaçu reportedly decreased by 90 percent.[27] However, according to Mauro de Brito, head of the Federal Revenue Secretariat office in Foz do Iguaçu, it will take several years for the customs integration between Paraguay and Brazil to yield the expected

---

[25]Sebastian Rotella, "Jungle Hub for World's Outlaws," *Los Angeles Times*, August 24, 1998, 1; and Ricardo Grinbaum, "In Paraguay, Smugglers' Paradise," *World Press Review*, 43, no.1 (January 1996), 25–26 (reprinted from *Veja*).

[26] Larry Rohter, "Terrorists Are Sought in Latin Smugglers' Haven," *New York Times*, September 27, 2001, A3.

[27] "Commerce between Ciudad del Este and Foz do Iguacu Drops by 90 Percent," *Vanguardia* [highest circulation daily in Ciudad del Este; aligned with the national daily *ABC Color*, it offers moderate and balanced reporting and editorial comment, but is occasionally sensationalistic], December 3, 2002, as translated for FBIS, "Brazil-Paraguay Triborder Press Highlights: November 25-29, 2002," December 3, 2002 (FBIS Document ID: LAP20021203000105).

results. Referring to Paraguay's "bribe culture," de Brito attributed this delay to differences in legislation and in "culture" of customs agents.[28]

In an attempt to curb the loss of tax revenues, Argentina imposed limits of US$100 per month on nondurable merchandise and US$150 per month on durables that can be purchased in the region. In a similar measure, Brazilian authorities reduced from US$500 to US$150 the monthly amount that the *sacoleiros* (small-time Brazilian importers) can spend in the region.[29] As a result of these and other measures, such as increased security, commercial activity in Ciudad del Este has declined considerably.[30]

Although Argentina's Puerto Iguazú traditionally has had the least economic activity of the three TBA cities, the greatly reduced traffic across the Tancredo Neves Bridge during the 1999-2000 period is also indicative of the economic downturn.[31] From 3.4 million people crossing in 1999, the number dropped to 1.4 million in 2000, while total vehicle passages declined from 350,751 in 1999 to 242,669 in 2000.[32] Argentine sources estimated in October 2001 that 120,000 people annually, or 4,000 daily, were crossing the Tancredo Neves Bridge.[33]

ILLICIT ACTIVITIES BY ISLAMIC TERRORIST GROUPS IN THE TBA

Background

The TBA cities of Ciudad del Este and Foz do Iguaçu have served as a base and a haven for Islamic terrorists for plotting and occasionally succeeding in carrying out terrorist attacks elsewhere in the Americas. Among the various Islamic fundamentalist groups reported to have a presence in the region are extremist cells tied to al Qaeda, Hizballah, Al-Jihad (Egyptian Islamic Jihad), and al-Muqawamah.

---

[28] "Brazil, Paraguay Border Customs Integration Facing Problems," *Vanguardia*, April 11, 2003, as translated by FBIS, "Highlights: Argentina-Brazil- Paraguay Triborder Media, April 11, 2003 (FBIS Document ID: LAP20030411000098).
[29] Bartolomé, 2.
[30] Bartolomé, 2.
[31] Bartolomé, 4, citing "Em Puerto Iguazú, a segurança é reforçada" [In Puerto Iguazú, Security Is Reinforced], *O Estado de São Paulo*, September 17, 2001.
[32] Mendel, William W., Foreign Military Studies Office (FMSO). "Paraguay's Ciudad del Este and the New Centers of Gravity," *Military Review* 82, no. 2 (March–April 2002), 51—58.
[33] Bartolomé, 2.

The bombing of the Israeli Embassy in Buenos Aires on March 17, 1992, followed by the bombing of a Jewish community center, the Argentine-Israeli Mutual Association (Asociación Mutual Israeli-Argentina—AMIA), a Jewish community center, in Buenos Aires on July 18, 1994, focused the attention of the TBA countries, Israel, and the United States on the TBA because the investigation into both attacks led back to Hizballah operatives in the TBA.[34] Since the Israeli Embassy bombing in 1992, Imad Mughniyah (also spelled Mughanniyah or Mugniyeh; alias 'Hajji'), a Lebanese national and the head of the security service of Al-Jihad (Egyptian Islamic Jihad), which is linked to the pro-Iranian Party of God, or Hizballah, has been a fugitive. In May 2003, Argentine prosecutors linked both Ciudad del Este and Foz do Iguaçu to the AMIA bombing and issued arrest warrants for two Lebanese citizens, Assad Ahmad Barakat (see Barakat, Assad Ahmad Mohamad, Appendix) and Imad Fayed Mugniyah, who at the time of the bombing were living in Ciudad del Este.[35] According to the investigators handling the AMIA case in Buenos Aires, Barakat played a crucial role in financing the bombing because he reportedly had a cell that made arrangements to import all of the materials related to the attack into the TBA. In the years since then, investigators have identified Barakat as not only Hizballah's military operations chief in the TBA, but also as its chief Southern Cone fund-raiser.[36]

It is not known what connection, if any, al Qaeda may have had with the AMIA attack, an action usually associated with Hizballah. Whether the AMIA bombing was collaboration

---

[34] Mario Daniel Montoya, "Israel Takes Special Interest in Triple Border Area," *Jane's Intelligence Review* 13, no. 12 (December 2001): 13–14; and Jack Epstein, "Where Tourism Meets Terrorism," *U.S. News & World Report* 117, no. 6 (August 8, 1994): 38.

[35] *ABC Color* [Internet version-www], May 28, 2003, as translated by FBIS Document ID: LAP20030528000104, "Argentine Prosecutors Link Tri-Border Hizballah Leaders to AMIA Attack," May 28, 2003.

[36] "Government Keeps Watchful Eye on Paraguay's Arab Community," October 13, 2001, EFE News Services (FBIS Rec. No. OEF2C4F9D99922F0).

between Hizballah and another group is unclear. Argentina's foreign ministry disclosed on October 18, 2001, that its embassy in Riyadh, Saudi Arabia, had received a telephone call on October 26, 2000, claiming responsibility for an unspecified "explosion" in Argentina. Argentine judicial sources believe that the callers to the Riyadh embassy were referring to the July 18, 1994, attack on the AMIA.[37] In late January 2003, Argentina's Secretariat for State Intelligence (Secretaría de Información del Estado—SIDE) presented President Eduardo Duhalde with a 500-page report on the AMIA bombing that confirms Hizballah's use of C4 plastic explosive, which arrived from Ciudad del Este along with the two or three suicide bombers, who came from Lebanon.[38] As of mid-2003, Argentine courts had resumed the investigation of the attacks on the AMIA and the Israeli Embassy in Buenos Aires and had determined that Assad Ahmad Barakat made suspicious trips to Teheran, Iran, between 1990 and 1991, and that he had also reportedly met with high-ranking officials of the Islamic Republic of Iran. On the same occasion, Barakat also traveled to Lebanon.[39]

The Islamic Terrorist Presence in the TBA, 1999-June 2003

There appears to be general agreement among U.S. counterterrorism officials that Islamic terrorist groups have a presence in the TBA, although some may be more skeptical than others that al Qaeda is included among these groups, much less cooperating with Hizballah in the region. Francis X. Taylor, the Department of State's coordinator for counterterrorism, told Congress on October 10, 2001, that the TBA has "...the longstanding presence of Islamic extremist organizations, primarily Hizballah, and, to a lesser extent, the Sunni extremist groups, such as the al-Gama'a al-Islamiyya (Egyptian Islamic Group) and Hamas."[40] Taylor noted that the activities of these organizations include fund-raising and proselytizing among the zone's Middle Eastern population, as well as document forging, money laundering, contraband

---

[37] "Al-Qaeda and Argentina," *Jane's Intelligence Digest*, October 26, 2001; Ed Blanche, "Al-Qaeda Link to Buenos Aires Bombings Emerges; Phone Call to Embassy in Riyadh Opens Can of Worms," *The Daily Star* [Beirut; Internet version-www], October 29, 2001, an transcribed by FBIS Document ID: GMP20011030000033, "Al-Qa'ida Link to Argentine Bombings Seen; Mughniyah 'Ordered out of Iran'," October 29, 2001.

[38] Raul Kollmann, "Report on Interview with an Unidentified 'Government Spokesman,'" *Pagina/12* [Buenos Aires; Internet version-www], January 19, 2003, as translated for FBIS, "Responsibility for Argentine-Jewish Center Bombing Attributed to Iran," January 19, 2003 (FBIS Document ID: LAP20030119000009).

[39] *ABC Color* [Internet version-www], June 9, 2003, as translated by FBIS Document ID: LAP20030609000051, "Paraguay: Argentine Courts Link Barakat to Iranian Leaders," June 9, 2003

[40] Anthony Faiola, "U.S. Terrorist Search Reaches Paraguay; Black Market Border Hub Called Key Finance Center for Middle East Extremists," *Washington Post*, October 13, 2001, A21.

smuggling, and weapons and drug trafficking. The U.S. Federal Bureau of Investigation (FBI) apparently shares that assessment. In the same hearing, a U.S. Congressman pointed out that "Open-source reporting indicates that the FBI claims that Islamic extremist cells linked with Hizballah, Islamic Jihad, and al Qaeda are operating in Paraguay, Uruguay, and Ecuador."[41] Mark Davidson, spokesman for the U.S. Embassy in Asunción, affirmed on May 22, 2002, that the TBA is indisputably an area from which Islamic terrorist groups are financed by means of money derived from illicit activities, but he, like Taylor, omitted mention of al Qaeda.

Al Qaeda reportedly has had an interest and a presence in the TBA since at least the mid-1990s. Osama bin Laden reportedly visited Foz do Iguaçu in 1995 (the specific month is unclear), according to *Veja*, a leading Brazilian newsweekly. *Veja*, citing an anonymous high official of the Brazilian Intelligence Agency (Agência Brasileira de Inteligência—Abin), reported that a 28-minute videotape shows bin Laden participating in meetings at a mosque in the area during his visit.[42] Al Qaeda's Khalid Sheikh Mohammed is also believed to have visited the TBA that December.[43] Mohammed also reportedly returned to the Foz do Iguaçu area in 1998.[44]

There have been indications that terrorist elements with possible al Qaeda connections have used mosques in the TBA for plotting or recruitment purposes. CNN reported that two

---

[41] "Prepared Statement of Representative Cass Ballenger, Chairman, Subcommittee on the Western Hemisphere, U.S. House of Representatives." Transcript of House Western Hemisphere Subcommittee Hearing, October 10, 2001. Center for International Policy, Columbia Project, http://www.ciponline.org/colombia/101001.htm.

[42] "Bin Laden Reportedly Spent Time in Brazil in '95," *Washington Post*, March 18, 2003, A24; "Bin Laden esteve em Foz do Iguaçu e até deu palestra em mesquita [Bin Laden Was in Foz do Iguaçu and Even Gave A Lecture in A Mosque], *O Estado de São Paulo*, March 16, 2003. [Estadao.com: http://www.estado.estadao.com.br/editorias/2003/03/16/int026.html]; and Policarpo Junior, "Ele esteve no Brasil" [He Was in Brazil], *Veja* on-line, no. 1,794 (March 19, 2003), http://veja.abril.com.br/190303/p_058.html.

[43] Reuters, "Bin Laden Reportedly Spent Time in Brazil in '95," *Washington Post*, March 18, 2003, A24; and *O Estado de São Paulo* [Internet version-www], March 9, 2003, as translated for FBIS, "Brazil: Terrorist Khalid Sheikh Mohamed's Passage Through Brazil Reported," March 9, 2003 (FBIS Document ID: LAP20030308000052); and *A Gazeta do Iguaçu,* March 10, 2003, 2, as translated for FBIS, "Brazilian Police: Khalid Shaykh Visit to Tri-border in 1995 Unconfirmed," March 10, 2003 (FBIS Document ID: LAP20030311000123).

[44] Kevin G. Hall, "Accused al-Qaida Terrorist Spent time in Brazil, Police Say," Knight Ridder Tribune News Service, March 13, 2003, 1.

mosques in Foz do Iguaçu and one in Ciudad del Este are reportedly suspected by international and regional intelligence sources of involvement in terrorist activity and serving as revolving doors for Islamic extremists.[45] Argentine intelligence documents show links between the mosques and various terror groups, including Hizballah and Egypt's al-Gama'a al-Islamiyya and Islamic Jihad.[46] Argentine security forces have identified Sheik Mounir Fadel, spiritual leader of Ciudad del Este's main mosque, as a senior Hizballah member.[47]

By mid-1999, the SIDE (Secretariat for State Intelligence) was investigating Islamic extremist groups in the TBA that allegedly were operating under the orders of Osama bin Laden.[48] The SIDE investigation resulted from a shared belief that Iran was no longer the only concern in regard to terrorist cells operating in Ciudad del Este and Foz do Iguaçu. That conviction was based on information from the SIDE's own files and from other intelligence services, which reported that bin Laden's al Qaeda had gained ground in the TBA as a result of Iran's partial withdrawal from the important Arab community in the area, thanks to Iranian President Mohamed Khatami.[49]

In 1999 SIDE agents began taping telephone calls made by Islamic extremists in Ciudad del Este and Foz do Iguaçu to the Middle East and secretly filming meetings of the Shi'ite and minority Sunni groups who were part of the huge Moslem population in the TBA.[50] As a result of this surveillance, the SIDE reported that al Qaeda agents had been identified in the TBA.[51] Coordinated police operations conducted in the three TBA cities on December 22, 1999, reportedly thwarted a plot by TBA-based terrorists under the control of Osama bin Laden and Hizballah leader Imad Mouniagh to stage simultaneous attacks on Jewish targets in Ciudad del Este, Buenos Aires, and Ottawa, Canada, in an attempt to undermine the Middle East peace

---

[45] Harris Whitbeck and Ingrid Arneson, "Sources: Terrorists Find Haven in South America," CNN, November 7, 2001, http://www.cnn.com/2001/WORLD/americas/11/07/inv.terror.south/index.html.

[46] Whitbeck and Arneson.

[47] Peter Hudson, "There Are No Terrorists Here," *Newsweek*, November 19, 2001.

[48] Daniel Santoro, *Clarín* [Buenos Aires; an Independent, tabloid-format daily; highest-circulation newspaper, Internet version], July 18, 1999, as translated for FBIS, "Bin Laden's Followers in Triborder Area Probed," July 19, 1999 (FBIS, WA1907180899).

[49] Santoro, *Clarín*.

[50] Daniel Santoro, *Clarín*, September 16, 2001, 8–9, as translated for FBIS, "Argentine Intelligence Services' 1999 Report on Usamah Bin-Ladin's Agents in Triborder Area Viewed," September 16, 2001 (FBIS LAP20010916000021).

[51] Mario Daniel Montoya, "War on Terrorism Reaches Paraguay's Triple Border," *Jane's Intelligence Review* 13, no. 12 (December 2001): 12; and Daniel Santoro, *Clarín*, September 16, 2001, 8–9, as translated for FBIS, "Argentine Intelligence Services' 1999 Report on Usamah Bin-Ladin's Agents in Triborder Area Viewed," September 16, 2001 (FBIS LAP20010916000021).

process.[52] Individuals rounded up but later released included operatives of Hamas and Hizballah, as well as a suspected Iranian intelligence agent. In order to escape the SIDE investigation, the top alleged Hizballah and al Qaeda agents involved—Hezballah's Assad Ahmad Barakat and the Muslim Brotherhood's or Al-Gama'a al-Islamiyya's Mohamed Ali Aboul-Ezz Al-Mahdi Ibrahim Soliman—reportedly left Ciudad del Este and Foz do Iguaçu, but both were later arrested.[53]

The SIDE also reported a significant shift in the Muslim terrorist groups in the TBA after 1999.[54] Pro-Iranian Shi'ite terrorist organizations, such as the Islamic Jihad and the Lebanese Hizballah faction, who had normally worked separately from the orthodox Sunnites and followed instructions from Iran, had begun to cooperate and maintain contact.[55] This shift appeared to follow factional infighting among moderate and radical Hizballah adherents in the TBA and perhaps suggested that al Qaeda had taken advantage of the tensions to recruit new acolytes.[56] As some of the influence of the Iranians and Hizballah on the various Islamic groups in the TBA faded, the smaller groups, according to the SIDE, began supporting bin Laden by collecting funds, indoctrinating others, giving refuge to fugitives, and offering basic military training, such as how to build homemade bombs.[57] The SIDE's reports reportedly were received with skepticism by the U.S. Central Intelligence Agency (CIA) and Israel's Mossad.[58]

One of the smaller Shi'ite extremist groups operating in the TBA is Al-Muqawamah al-Islamiyah, or Islamic Resistance. The shadowy Al-Muqawamah appears to be a principal pro-Iran section of Hizballah whose members live normal lives in sleeper cells but become

---

[52] Special Correspondents Vladimir Jara Vera and Dany Ortiz, *ABC Color* [Asunción; Internet version; major daily, opposed to the González Macchi administration; owner Aldo Zuccolillo is an influential Oviedo Supporter of former General Oviedo], December 23, 1999, as translated for FBIS, "Police Conduct Operation to Intimidate Islamic Extremists,",December 23, 1999 (FBIS ID: FTS19991223001521).

[53] Jara Vera and Dany Ortiz, *ABC Color*.

[54] Tânia Monteiro, DPA, EFE, and Agence France Presse, "Tríplice fronteira tinha agentes sauditas, diz "Clarín" [TriBorder has Saudi agents, *Clarín* says], Estadão Web site, September 17, 2001.

[55] Daniel Santoro, *Clarín* [Internet version], July 18, 1999, as translated for FBIS, "Bin Laden's Followers in Triborder Area Probed," July 19, 1999 (FBIS, WA1907180899).

[56] Comp. A. William Samii, "Competition Among South American Hizballah Resumes," *Iran Report* [RFE/RL] 3, no. 27 (July 17, 2000), citing *ABC Color*, July 12, 2000; *Iran Report* [RFE/RL], January 10, 2000; and "Competition Among South American Hizballah," RFE/RL, February 6, 2002, translating *ABC Color*, January 5, 2002, http://www.rferl.org/iran-report/2000/01/2-100100.html.

[57] Daniel Santoro, *Clarín*, September 16, 2001, 8–9, as translated for FBIS, "Argentine Intelligence Services' 1999 Report on Usamah Bin-Ladin's Agents in Triborder Area Viewed," September 16, 2001 (FBIS LAP20010916000021).

[58] Santoro.

combatants when mobilized.[59] In early 2000, Brazilian and Paraguayan experts obtained photographs of Arab extremists taken at the Al-Mukawama training camp (see Fayad, Sobhi Mahmoud, Appendix), possibly located at a farm outside Foz do Iguaçu.[60] The men in the photos included several businessmen. They were photographed beside an Iranian flag and a flag from al-Muqawamah, a shadowy pro-Iran wing of Hizballah. Another photograph is said to show a Hizballah leader reading a letter from Imad Mounigh, presumably wanted Hizballah activist Imad Mughniyah.[61] Argentine intelligence officials reportedly believe that Hizballah runs weekend training camps on farms in the remote jungle terrain near Foz do Iguaçu, where young adults are recruited and given weapons training and children are indoctrinated in Hizballah ideology.[62]

In late 2000, at least one known TBA-based terrorist was involved in a plot to attack the U.S. and Israeli embassies in Asunción along with 30 other Islamic terrorists, who would carry out diversionary attacks elsewhere in the city in order to distract security forces.[63] On November 28, 2000, Paraguayan authorities arrested Salah Abdul Karim Yassine, a Palestinian and suspected Hamas explosives expert who had entered the country using false documents and was living in Ciudad del Este.[64] Yassine was being investigated for his suspected affiliation with an Egyptian terrorist organization.[65] It was found that he was involved in the plot, and he was sentenced

---

[59] Sami G. Hajjar, *Hizballah: Terrorism, National Liberation, or Menace?* Carlisle, Pennsylvania: Strategic Studies Institute, U.S. Army War College, August 2002, http://216.239.57.100/search?q=cache:11y-v-VhCqYJ:www.carlisle.army.mil/ssi/pubs/2002/hizbala/hizbala.pdf+al-Muqawamah&hl=en&ie=UTF-8.

[60] *ABC Color* [Internet version-www], January 16, 2002, as translated for FBIS, "Paraguay: Court Investigates Hizballah Base Photos" (FBIS, LAP20020116000091).

[61] London Bureau Roundup of Terrorism Issues/Developments in the Mideast/Islamic World and the Aegean derived from sources monitored by FBIS, "Latin America: Islamic Fundamentalists in Colombia, Paraguay," January 10, 2002 (FBIS GMP20020109000400).

[62] Jeffrey Goldberg, "In the Party of God," *The New Yorker* 79, no. 32 (October 28, 2002).

[63] Bartolomé, 11, citing "Un presunto jefe de grupo terrorista árabe fue detenido" [A presumed head of an Arab terrorist group was detained], *Noticias*, November 30, 2000.

[64] *Patterns of Global Terrorism, 2000*, Office of the Coordinator for Counterterrorism, April 30, 2001; Nelson Fredy Padilla, "Los hombres de Osama bin Laden en Colombia" [The Men of Osama bin Laden in Colombia] *Cromos*, No. 4, 364, September 24, 2001; and Pedro Doria, "Terrorismo aqui no lado" (Terrorism Here Next Door), www.No.com.br, November 30, 2000.

[65] Bartolomé, 11.

to a four-year prison term on charges of possessing false documents and entering the country illegally.

Despite increased surveillance by security forces in the region, the TBA is probably still used by Islamic terrorist groups as a fund-raising center and as a base for plotting, coordinating, or otherwise supporting terrorist attacks against U.S. and Israeli targets in the Americas. Al Qaeda operatives in the TBA reportedly were connected to a foiled al Qaeda plot to simultaneously attack the U.S. embassies in Montevideo, Uruguay, and Quito, Ecuador, in April 2001.[66] On October 10, 2001, a group of ten terrorists identified as belonging to a Lebanese Hizballah cell was reportedly caught in Mexico City on its way to assassinate President Vicente Fox and carry out a terrorist attack in the Mexican Senate.[67] The terrorists reportedly reached Mexico from the TBA, following a training session. The description of one of the instructors resembled Imad Mughniyah, who, working from his bases in Iran and Hizballah-controlled areas of Lebanon, reportedly directs the activities of Islamic terrorists in South America, including the TBA, in coordination with al Qaeda.[68]

U.S. authorities expressed concern in late 2001 over the possibility that lax immigration procedures in various Latin American countries have allowed terrorist "sleepers" to adopt new identities and to infiltrate into the United

---

[66] Jose Meirelles Passos, "The Shadow of Bin Ladin in Latin America," *O Globo* [Rio de Janeiro; Internet version-www], October 29, 2001, as translated for FBIS, "Brazil: Daily Notes US Views Triborder as Al-Qa'idah Center for L.A.," October 29, 2001 (FBIS LAP20011029000036).

[67] DEBKAfile Exclusive, "New Direction in Search for Anthrax Culprit" [Jerusalem; DEBKAfile www], November 11, 2001, as transcribed by FBIS, "DEBKA Sources Say Iraqi Nuclear Devices Ready for Arming, View Bin Ladin Threat," November 11, 2001 (FBIS Document ID: MP20011111000147).

[68] Mike Boettcher, "South America's 'Tri-border' Back on Terrorism Radar," CNN, November 8, 2002, citing "coalition intelligence sources," http://www.cnn.com/2002/WORLD/americas/11/07/terror.triborder/. For discussions of al Qaeda-Hizballah links, see Yael Shahar, ICT Researcher, "Al-Qa'ida Links to Iranian Security Services," Herzliyya International Policy Institute for Counterterrorism [Tel Aviv; Internet version-www], January 20, 2003; and Lenny Ben-David, "Sunni and Shiite Terrorist Networks: Competition or Collusion?" *Jerusalem Issue Brief*, Jerusalem Center for Public Affairs [Jerusalem; Internet version-www], December 18, 2002, as transcribed by FBIS, "Israeli Expert Says International Terror Breaches Secular-Religious Divide," December 18, 2002 (FBIS Document ID: GMP20021225000066).

States, especially from Argentina. By 2001, investigators had come to believe that numerous Islamic terrorist "sleeper cells" had been established in Ciudad del Este and Foz do Iguaçu, as well as Uruguay's Chuy since the 1990s.[69] Based on an examination of telephone records, Argentine investigators in 2002 found "evidence of coordination between the TBA and sleeper cells in Buenos Aires." Two main centers of activity were cited: the principal mosque in Foz do Iguaçu and a travel agency there.[70]

Paraguay's Vice Interior Minister Mario Agustin Sapriza affirmed on May 3, 2001, that the TBA serves as a base of operations for dormant Islamic extremist cells linked to international terrorism.[71] Sapriza explained that Hizballah, Hamas, and other terrorist organizations use this region to plan their actions, to obtain supplies, and to live for a certain period of time before launching new attacks in other countries.

Argentina and Brazil have been less forthcoming in acknowledging the existence of sleeper cells in the TBA. Brazil's Justice Minister José Gregori said in October 2001 that he had no "conclusive information" on al Qaeda cells in Brazil.[72] However, Judge Walter Fanganiello Maierovitch, a money-laundering expert affiliated with the Giovanni Falconi Brazilian Criminal Sciences Institute, expressed an opposite viewpoint regarding al Qaeda in making the following points in a September 2001 *O Globo* interview:[73]

❖ al Qaeda is establishing a base in the Arab community near Ciudad del Este.

❖ bin Laden is attempting to establish a presence in the TBA because al Qaeda's terrorist activities are linked with the trafficking of arms, drugs, and uranium, as well as money laundering, in association with the Russian and Chinese mafias.

❖ bin Laden's goal is to use religious entities as fronts for training terrorists and provide a hiding place for Islamic fugitives.

---

[69] Bartolomé, 10, citing "Divergencias nas relações Brasília-Washington" (Differences in relations between Brasilia and Washington], *Zero Hora*, September 19, 2001; and *La Nación* [Buenos Aires], October 3, 2001, as translated for FBIS, "National Border Guard Commander: Tri-Border Area Hotbed of Sleeper Cells," October 3, 2001 (FBIS Docoument ID: LAP20011003000015).

[70] Larry Rohter, "South America Region Under Watch for Signs of Terrorists," *New York Times*, December 15, 2002, 1A, 32.

[71] *ABC Color* [Internet version-www], May 4, 2001, as translated for FBIS, "Paraguay: Vice Interior Minister Confirms Presence of 'Dormant Islamic Terrorist Cells'" (FBIS Document ID: LAP20010505000002).

[72] José Meirelles Passos, "The Shadow of Bin Ladin in Latin America," *O Globo* [Internet version-www], October 29, 2001, as translated for FBIS, "Brazil: Daily Notes US Views Triborder as Al-Qa'idah Center for L.A.," October 29, 2001 (FBIS Document ID: LAP20011029000036).

[73] Germano Oliveira, *O Globo*, September 19, 2001, as translated for FBIS, "Brazil's Former Drug Czar: Bin-Ladin Establishing Al-Qa'idah Cell on Triborder," September 19, 2001 (FBIS Document ID: LAP200109119000051).

❖ bin Laden is recruiting members of the Hizballah group that bombed the Jewish community center (AMIA) in Buenos Aires in 1994.

In early 2002, further suggesting al Qaeda's presence in the TBA, the Paraguayan press reported that al Qaeda and other Islamic terrorist groups had established training camps and were talking of holding a secret terrorist summit meeting in the TBA.[74] In early February, Paraguayan and foreign security forces as well as Brazilian, Argentine, Israeli, and U.S. agents searched the TBA, especially Ciudad del Este and Foz do Iguaçu, for five Afghan citizens who allegedly belong to the Taliban and are linked to al Qaeda, either as supporters or members.[75] Each of the individuals allegedly was carrying three or four sets of different identity documents. Adding to concerns that Osama bin Laden's operatives were among those operating in the TBA, a map of the TBA was recovered from an al Qaeda safehouse in Kabul, Afghanistan in 2002.[76]

One individual suspected of being linked to Osama bin Laden's al Qaeda is Egyptian citizen Al-Mahdi Ibrahim Soliman, who was arrested on April 15, 2002, in Foz do Iguaçu, where he had been

---

[74] Larry Rohter, "South America Region Under Watch for Signs of Terrorists," *New York Times*, December 15, 2002, 1A, 32

[75]*ABC Color* Web site, February 5, 2002, as cited by "International Security Forces Search for Five Afghan Fugitives in Paraguay," BBC Monitoring Service [UK], February 5, 2002.

[76] Larry Rohter, "South America Region Under Watch for Signs of Terrorists," *New York Times*, December 15, 2002, 1A, 32

living for seven years.[77] He was arrested under charges filed by the Egyptian government that he is a member of a terrorist faction, namely Al-Gama'a al-Islamiyya, that carried out deadly attacks in several countries. Soliman earlier had been arrested in Foz do Iguaçu in 1999 on charges of dealing in contraband merchandise.[78]

In April 2002, Paraguayan reporters linked Assad Ahmad Barakat to Osama bin Laden by pointing out that Barakat was the owner of the Mondial (World) Engineering and Construction company, with offices in Ciudad del Este and Beirut. This company was suspected of having made contributions to al Qaeda, using money obtained from real estate fraud.[79] Barakat was allegedly using the company to collect funds for al Qaeda by selling apartments in Beirut.[80] For example, unidentified intelligence sources cited an authorization by Barakat, dated February 14, 2002, in Foz do Iguaçu ordering the transfer of an apartment for US$120,000 in Lebanon.[81] Other unspecified front businesses created by Barakat are reportedly designed to channel funds to Osama bin Laden, under the pretext of charitable contributions to orphanages. Journalist Sebastian Junger, citing unidentified Argentine intelligence sources, reported in late 2000 that Ramzi bin al-Shibh, the al Qaeda leader who was arrested in Pakistan in 2002, "has known, confirmed contacts with a Lebanese businessman working in Ciudad del Este, Paraguay, and in Foz do Iguaçu, Brazil."[82] Whether Ramzi bin al-Shibh, who is in U.S. custody, has identified this businessman as Assad Ahmad Barakat is not known.

In July 2002, the Paraguayan police arrested a pair of Lebanese men, Ali Nizar Darhoug, owner of two shops in Ciudad del Este, and his nephew, Muhammad Daoud Yassine, who were said to be raising funds for al Qaeda. Ali Nizar Darhoug's name was reportedly found in an address book belonging to Abu Zubaydah, one of the highest-ranking al Qaeda officials to be

---

[77] Mauri Konig, "Egípcio preso em Foz do Iguaçu" [Egyptian Arrested in Foz do Iguaçu], *O Estado de São Paulo*, April 16, 2002, http://www.estado.estadao.com.br/editorias/2002/04/16/int002.html; and Miriam Karam, *São Paulo Valor* [financial daily, published jointly by the Folha and Globo media conglomerates; Internet version-www], May 20, 2002, as translated for FBIS, "Brazil: Federal Police Denies Presence of Terrorist Cells in Foz do Iguaçu," (FBIS Document ID: LAP20020520000040).

[78] AJB, "Terrorismo: Egípcio é capturado pela PF" [Terrorism: Egyptian Is Captured by PF], *Correiro Braziliense* [Brasília], April 16, 2002, http://www2.correioweb.com.br/cw/EDICAO_20020416/pri_ult_160402_259.htm.

[79] Bartolomé, 16, citing "Triple frontera: Empresa sería de Al-Qaeda" [Triborder: Company is linked to al Qaeda], *Ámbito Financiero*, April 30, 2002, 14.

[80] "Barakat Continues To Collect For Hizballah," *Última Hora* [Asunción], May 1, 2002, as translated by FBIS, "Highlights: Paraguay Press," May 1, 2002 (FBIS Document ID: LAP20020501000022).

[81] "Barakat Continues To Collect For Hizballah," *Última Hora* [Asunción], May 1, 2002.

[82] Sebastian Junger, "Terrorism's New Geography," *Vanity Fair*, no. 508 (December 2002): 196.

captured by the United States.[83] Darhoug was wiring as much as US$80,000 each month to banks in the United States, the Middle East, and Europe.[84]

A spike in reports of al Qaeda in the TBA took place in October 2002. Argentina bolstered security measures in the region after several reports from Israel's intelligence service, the Mossad, warned of the presence of al Qaeda and Hizballah cells in Ciudad del Este.[85] In late October 2002, Argentine intelligence informed the United States of an al Qaeda-Hizballah meeting that was held in the TBA. A CNN report of November 8, citing "coalition intelligence sources," also disclosed that a "terrorist summit to plan attacks against U.S. and Israeli targets in the Western hemisphere" had taken place in Ciudad del Este and the surrounding area, and that the terrorists attending the meetings were representatives of Hizballah and organizations sympathetic to the al Qaeda network.[86] CNN's Middle East intelligence sources also indicated a new terrorist effort aimed at U.S. and Israeli interests and coordinated by Imad Mughniyah. CNN reported that Mughniyah, working from his bases in Iran and Hizballah-controlled areas of Lebanon, was directing the activities of terrorists in South America and planning to hit U.S. and Israeli targets if the United States attacked Iraq, or if Israel was drawn into the conflict. The Paraguayan government denied the CNN report.[87] Argentine intelligence sources reportedly also rejected the CNN report that the meeting was held in the TBA, claiming instead that it was held in another Latin American location.[88]

---

[83] Jeffrey Goldberg, "In the Party of God," *The New Yorker* 79, no. 32 (October 28, 2002).

[84] Goldberg; and Larry Rohter, "South America Region Under Watch for Signs of Terrorists," *New York Times*, December 15, 2002, 1A, 32

[85] *Clarín* [Buenos Aires; Internet version-www], October 19, 2002, as translated by FBIS, "Argentina: Newspapers Publish Contradictory Reports On Possible Attacks In Tri-Border Area," October 19, 2002 (FBIS Document ID: LAP20021019000022).

[86] Mike Boettcher, with Ingrid Arnesen, "South America's 'Tri-border' Back on Terrorism Radar," CNN, November 8, 2002, http://www.cnn.com/2002/WORLD/americas/11/07/terror.triborder/.

[87] "Cabinet Members Refute TV Report and Deny Existence of Terrorist Activities," *Vanguardia* [Ciudad del Este], November 9, 2002, as translated for FBIS, "Highlights: Brazil - Paraguay Triborder Press 4-15 Nov 02," November 21, 2002 (FBIS Document ID: LAP20021121000006).

[88] *La Nación* [Buenos Aires], November 8, 2002, 3, as translated by FBIS, "Argentine Intelligence Services Dismiss Report on Terrorist Powwow as Inaccurate," November 8, 2002 (FBIS Document ID: LAP20021108000038).

The potential for TBA-based terrorists acquiring powerful explosives was illustrated by an incident reported on June 4, 2003, when Alto Paraná Police recovered all nine boxes of dynamite stolen from a quarry in Hernandarias, a town neighboring Ciudad del Este, over the previous weekend. Police observed members of a well-known gang formed by Brazilian and Paraguayan criminals hanging around the neighborhood where four individuals were arrested. Given the destructive potential of the material, which was powerful enough to destroy the Friendship Bridge, police believed that the explosives could have been sold to terrorists.[89]

Terrorist Fund-Raising in the TBA

Narcotics Trafficking

A topic in itself, narcotics trafficking in the TBA, as it relates to the Lebanese Mafia, can only be briefly summarized here. It is clearly a major activity of the Islamic terrorist groups and organized crime syndicates operating in the region. With lax border controls and more than 100 hidden airstrips in the region, the TBA has long been popular with contraband smugglers, gunrunners, and drug traffickers. A large number of small airplanes take off from clandestine airstrips in Paraguayan territory and enter Brazilian air space. Many of them also cross Argentina's Misiones Province. The TBA is reportedly a conduit for the smuggling of some drugs through Argentina, Brazil, and Paraguay, which serve as transit countries for Andean cocaine (see Fig. 2, Drug-Trafficking Routes in the Tri-Border Area (TBA), Appendix).[90] One route on the Bolivia-Paraguay-Brazil corridor goes through Ciudad del Este and Foz do Iguaçu to the ports of Paranaguá, Santos, and Rio de Janeiro on the Atlantic coast of Brazil.[91]

Despite the significant smuggling activity in the region, the TBA's importance as a drug-smuggling conduit may have declined in recent years as a result of increased surveillance by security forces of the three TBA countries. The great majority of the cocaine smuggled out of Paraguay leaves the country through border towns to the north of the TBA (Pedro Juan Caballero

---

[89] "Police Recover Explosives, Robbers Arrested," *Vanguardia* [Ciudad del Este], June 4, 2003, as translated by FBIS, Tri-Border Media Highlights, June 4, 2003 (FBIS Document ID: LAP20030604000111).

[90] U.S. Department of State, *International Narcotics Control Strategy Report –2002*. Washington, DC: Bureau for International Narcotics and Law Enforcement Affairs, March 2003, http://www.state.gov/g/inl/rls/nrcrpt/2002/html/ 17952pf.htm. Paraguay is a transit country for between 40 and 60 metric tons of Colombian, Bolivian and Peruvian cocaine that traverses its territory destined for Argentina, Brazil, the United States, Europe, and Africa, according to the *International Narcotics Control Strategy Report –2002*, http://www.state.gov/g/inl/rls/nrcrpt/2002/html/ 17944.htm.

[91] "Brasil," http://www.ogd.org/rapport/gb/RP12_4_BRESIL.html.

and Capitán Bado) and to the south of the TBA (Posadas). Apparently for this reason, drug-related border arrests at Puerto Iguazú have declined since 2000.[92] Capitán Bado is a center for the production of marijuana and distribution of cocaine. The marijuana is transported to Brazil by land; most of the cocaine is flown in clandestine flights aboard small aircraft.[93] Posadas is just across the Río Paraná from Encarnación, which has a large Arab population and is known as a main contraband center.

Despite the TBA's relatively limited role as a drug-smuggling conduit, there is no question that narcotics trafficking remains a major activity in the region, and the Hizballah network and the Lebanese Mafia in general are heavily involved in it. Lebanese citizen Ali Assi was captured at Beirut's airport with a 10-kilo shipment of cocaine in his two suitcases in May 2002. Assi had recently taken charge of running a coffee shop in the Islamic Welfare Center in Ciudad del Este.[94] Assi is the father-in-law of Ali Hassan Abdallah (also known as Ali Asan Abadia and "Alito"), who was, together with Assad Barakat, one of the principal coordinators of a Hizballah financial network in the TBA. Ali Hassan Abdallah had also been a trade partner in Ciudad del Este of convicted Hizballah figure Sobhi Mahmoud Fayad.[95] In May 2002, Ali Hassan Abdallah was considered a fugitive. By early March 2003, he had been expelled from Angola and was believed to be ordering electronic funds transfers (EFTs) to Islamic extremist groups in the Middle East through his nephew, Rayan Hussein Abdallah, in Ciudad del Este.[96]

---

[92] Mendel, citing Gendarmería National, *Escuadrón 13 'Iguazú': Estadísticas del funcionamiento del escuadrón 13 'Iguazu'*. Puerto de Iguazú, Argentina: Gendarmería National, September 2001.

[93] Clarinha Glock, "Brazil-Paraguay: A Full Plate for Journalists," Inter American Press Association, July 19, 2001, http://www.impunidad.com/atrisk/brasil_paraguay7_19_01E.html.

[94] *ABC Color* [Internet version-www], May 28, 2002, as translated for FBIS, "Paraguay: Daily Reports More Evidence of Barakat's Contributions to Hizballah," May 28, 2002 (FBIS Document ID: LAP20020528000073).

[95] *Vanguardia* [Ciudad del Este; Internet version-www], May 23, 2002, "Paraguay: Triborder Daily Says US Has Not Shown Evidence Against Alleged Terrorist," May 23, 2002 (FBIS Document ID: LAP20020523000084); and "Paraguay: Lebanese Merchant Sought in Paraguay Expelled from Angola," BBC Monitoring Americas – Political [London], March 14, 2003, citing *ABC Color* Website, March 14, 2003.

[96] *ABC Color* [Internet version-www], March 14, 2003, citing "high-ranking" local police intelligence sources, in collaboration with their counterparts in Lebanon and the TBA, as translated by FBIS, "Paraguay Press Highlights," March 14, 2003 (FBIS Document ID: LAP20030314000106); and *ABC Color*, March 13, 2003, as translated by FBIS, "Angola Ousts Lebanese Fugitive Linked to Hizballah From Paraguay," March 13, 2003 (FBIS Document ID: LAP20030313000120).

Hizballah and the Lebanese Mafia continue to use Foz do Iguaçu and Ciudad del Este as transit points for smuggling Colombian cocaine. The arrest of an alleged Lebanese Mafia ringleader in São Paulo in January 2003 exposed an operation that was moving between 400 and 1,000 kilos of Colombian cocaine per month via Foz do Iguaçu, where it was then shipped to São Paulo.[97] A prominent Lebanese businessman, Bassam Naboulsi, who resides in the TBA and is a cousin of Assad Ahmad Barakat, was arrested on January 29, 2003, in São Paulo, Brazil. Bassam Naboulsi was accused of ties with a group of drug traffickers, one of whose members, also residing in Ciudad del Este, was arrested in Beirut the week before.[98] Bassam Naboulsi's brother, Hassan Naboulsi, owns Hassan Internacional, located in Ciudad del Este's Page shopping gallery. The operation led to the arrest of 14 men belonging to what the PF (Federal Police) refers to as the "Barakat clan," among them Akram Farhat, who is the brother-in-law of well-known Ciudad del Este businessman Samir Jebai. PF authorities believe that this group, led by Assad Barakat from within the Brasília prison, could be shipping cocaine to Middle Eastern and European markets.

On May 10, 2003, Hassan Abdallah Dayoub, a Lebanese merchant who lives in Ciudad del Este, was arrested at Asunción's Silvio Pettirossi Airport, while in possession of 2.3 kilos of cocaine hidden in an electric piano. High-ranking police sources connected with the investigation of Dayoub reportedly believe that his arrest constitutes overwhelming proof that Barakat's Hizballah clan has a "wing of narcotraffickers."[99] This is because Dayoub is a cousin of Barakat. Investigators believe that Barakat himself hired Dayoub as a "mule" to market the drug in Damascus, Syria. Once in the Argentine capital, Dayoub intended to transfer to an Iberia flight to Madrid, whence he would proceed on to his final destination of Damascus.

Other Fund-Raising Activities

In addition to the estimated US$60 to US$100 million per year that it receives from Iran, Hizballah reportedly has also relied extensively on funding from the Shi'ite Lebanese Diaspora in

---

[97] Marcelo Godoy, *O Estado de São Paulo* [Internet Version-www], January 24, 2003, as translated by FBIS, "Brazil: Lebanese Mafia Members in São Paulo Arrested, Drugs Seized," January 24, 2003 (FBIS Document ID: LAP20030124000070).

[98] "Brazilian Police Arrest Lebanese Citizen," *ABC Color* [Internet version-www], January 30, 2003, as translated for FBIS, January 30, 2003 (FBIS Document ID: LAP20030130000073).

[99] *ABC Color* [Internet version-www], May 12, 2003, as translated by FBIS, "Paraguayan Police Make Arrest , Seize Cocaine From Tri-border Hizballah Head's Cousin," May 12, 2003 (FBIS Document ID: LAP20030512000065).

West Africa, the United States, and most importantly the TBA.[100] Islamic money laundering in the TBA is concealed by the common practice of the local Arab community of remitting funds to relatives in the Middle East. Some of these remittances are suspected of being directed to Arab terrorist organizations, particularly Hizballah.[101] In late 2002, Argentine officials linked Lebanese terrorists in the TBA with money laundering, counterfeiting of U.S. dollars, and other illicit financial activities. As evidence, they cited "thousands of U.S. dollars bearing stamps from Lebanese currency exchange banks, tens of thousands of dollars in phony bills, and receipts from wire transfers made between the tri-border area and the Middle East."[102]

Argentina's Ramón Mestre, director of the Permanent Work Group (Grupo de Trabajo Permanente—GTP), founded to establish a coordinated common policy against terrorism in the countries that make up Mercosur (Common Market of the South), said in early December 2001 that the TBA had given "logistical support to terrorist organizations by providing money to groups that operate in other parts of the world." He said that activities such as the illegal traffic of immigrants and drug trafficking in the region "are elements that are in some way linked to terrorism...."[103]

Brazilian authorities have estimated that more than US$6 billion a year in illegal funds is laundered in the TBA. Every evening, a dozen armored trucks loaded with laundered money leave Ciudad del Este for Foz do Iguaçu, the Brazilian town on the opposite side of the border. Paraguay's Finance Ministry issued an order in January 2003 to suspend sending of dollars abroad, but a reporter found that it was apparently not being applied to armored vans or trucks leaving the TBA. One van known to be was carrying reais and dollars was observed crossing the Friendship Bridge into Brazil on January 20, 2003.[104]

During the 1999-2001 period, Islamic extremist groups, specifically Hizballah and Hamas, received a total of between US$50 million and US$500 million from Arab residents of

---

[100] Blanca Madani, "Hezbollah's Global Finance Network: The Triple Frontier," *Middle East Intelligence Bulletin* [a monthly publication of the United States Committee for a Free Lebanon] 4, no. 1 (January 2002).

[101] Bartolomé, 9.

[102] Mike Boettcher, with Ingrid Arnesen, "South America's 'Tri-border' Back on Terrorism Radar," CNN, November 8, 2002, http://www.cnn.com/2002/WORLD/americas/11/07/terror.triborder/.

[103] *El País* [Montevideo], December 1, 2001, translated in "Uruguay Press Highlights," December 3, 2001 (FBIS Document ID: LAP20011203000074).

[104] "Paraguay: Lack of Control System on Border with Brazil Allows Currency Flight," BBC Monitoring Americas – Political [London], January 23, 2003, 1, citing *ABC Color* Web site, January 22, 2003.

Foz do Iguaçu through Paraguayan financial institutions.[105] An investigation begun in September 2001 also determined that a group of 42 Arabs in Ciudad del Este remitted abroad, mostly to Lebanon, approximately US$50 million, apparently during the 1997-2001 period. It is believed that these funds were derived from arms trafficking and other illicit activities.[106]

Argentine police and regional security organizations in general have described the Page shopping center, located in Ciudad del Este, as the regional command post for Hizballah. They have also linked Barakat to a Brazilian mosque that the police also described as a central Hizballah meeting place.[107] On September 12, 2001, a Paraguayan SWAT team raided Assad Ahmad Barakat's closet-sized shop, Casa Apollo, in this arcade. Barakat, who was away on business, escaped arrest. The police confiscated more than 60 hours of videotapes and CD-ROMs that show military marches and attacks with explosives in various parts of the world.[108] The confiscated material also included professional training courses for suicide bombers. The SWAT team also seized boxes containing financial statements totaling US$250,000 in monthly transfers to the Middle East and descriptions of at least 30 recent attacks in Israel and the Israeli-occupied territories.[109] The four principal individuals involved in the money remittance operations that were uncovered in September 2001 were Assad Ahmad Barakat and three of his principal Hizballah lieutenants in the Casa Apollo shop—Sobhi Mahmoud Fayad, Mazen Ali Saleh, and Salhed Mahmoud Fayad (Sobhi's brother).[110] Paraguayan prosecutor Carlos Cálcena noted that Barakat and Saleh sent money to international terrorist bank accounts in various countries. Specifically, they sent half a million dollars to Canada, Chile, and the United States (New York), and banks drafts of US$524,000 to Lebanon. Paraguayan Police found a letter from the Hizballah commander congratulating Barakat for financing activities in the Middle East.[111]

---

[105] Roberto Cosso, "Extremistas receberam US$50 mi de Foz do Iguaçu" (Extremists Received US$50 million from Foz do Iguaçu), *Folha de S. Paulo*, December 3, 2001.

[106] Bartolomé, 9, citing "Arabes envían US$50 milliones al exterior" [Arabs Send US$50 Million Abroad], October 3, 2001.

[107] Jose de Cordoba, "Is Jungle Junction a Terrorist Hideaway?—In Nexus of Latin Nations Is Casbah...and More, Say the Local Police," *Wall Street Journal*, November 28, 2001, A10.

[108] José Maschio, "Paraguayan Court Evidence Cited on Hizballah Link at Triborder," *Folha de São Paulo* [Internet version-www], November 26, 2001 (FBIS LAP20011126000074); and Stan Lehman, "Wanted by Paraguay, Hezbollah Supporter Is Free in Brazilian Town Across the Border," AP, December 12, 2001.

[109] Anthony Faiola, "U.S. Terrorist Search Reaches Paraguay; Black Market Border Hub Called Key Finance Center for Middle East Extremists," *Washington Post*, October 13, 2001, A21.

[110] Godoy, *O Estado de São Paulo*.

[111] Ricardo Galhardo Enviado, "Paraguai pede a prisão de libanês no Brasil" [Paraguay Sentences a Lebanese in Brazil to Prison], *O Globo*, November 6, 2001.

Argentine police also claimed that Barakat was involved in distributing US$60 million in counterfeit U.S. dollars printed in Colombia.[112]

On October 2, 2001, Mazen Ali Saleh and Salhed Mahmoud Fayad, both in their 20s, were arrested in Ciudad del Este, in possession of documents indicating regular remittances of between US$25,000 and US$50,000 to suspected Muslim radicals. Both were linked to Assad Ahmad Barakat.[113] The following day, Paraguayan police raided Casa Apollo for the second time in three weeks and this time arrested Barakat. Nevertheless, he escaped from prison and fled to Brazil, where, as a Brazilian citizen, he was not considered to be a security threat, at least until June 22, 2002, when he was arrested at his home in Foz do Iguaçu and imprisoned in Brasília. Barakat's business and Hizballah partner, Salman Reda, who fled jail on the same day in October 2001 as Barakat, was charged in Argentina with transporting explosives used against the Israeli Embassy in Buenos Aires in 1992.[114]

Sobhi Mahmoud Fayad was arrested in Ciudad del Este in late October 2001, after the prosecutor's office found documents at Barakat's shop indicating that Fayad had transferred large sums of money to banks in Lebanon and Canada.[115] Brazilian security agencies claimed that the financial aid offered in 2000 by groups in the TBA to Islamic and Middle Eastern terrorist organizations, such as Hizballah, Hamas, and the Islamic Jihad, totaled US$261 million.[116] Intelligence reports sent by Brazil to Paraguayan authorities between late 1999 and early 2000 reportedly mention three Hizballah leaders with whom Barakat allegedly met during trips to Lebanon that were at least annual.[117]

In late 2001, the Paraguayan intelligence services, which were collecting information on the activities of Lebanese citizens living in the TBA, reportedly found more evidence on how Barakat collected money for Hizballah. According to the evidence, he used blackmail and even

---

[112] Cordoba, *Wall Street Journal*.

[113] "Government Keeps Watchful Eye on Paraguay's Arab Community," October 13, 2001, EFE News Services (FBIS Rec. No. OEF2C4F9D99922F0).

[114] Roberto Godoy, *O Estado de São Paulo* [São Paulo; Internet version-www], November 12, 2001, as translated for FBIS, "Brazil: Foreign Intelligence Agents Spying on Triborder Mosques," November 12, 2001 (FBIS Document ID: LAP20011112000016).

[115] Kevin G. Hall, "Alleged Fund-Raiser for Hezbollah Arrested in Paraguay," Night Ridder/Tribune News Service, November 1, 2002, K7344.

[116] Riyadh Alam-al-Din, "Washington Begins the War on Hizballah in the Border Triangle," *Al-Watan al-Arabi* [Paris], December 21, 2001, 18–19, as translated for FBIS, "Report Says US Antiterror Campaign To Target Hizballah Network in S. America" (FBIS Document ID: GMP20011221000179).

[117] Roberto Cosso, "Brazil: $50 Million Remitted to Terrorist Groups from Triborder Area," *Folha de São Paulo* [Internet version-www], December 3, 2001, as translated by FBIS, December 3, 2001 (FBIS Document ID: LAP20011203000110.

death threats to force other Lebanese citizens to contribute to the Muslim fundamentalist group.[118] In 2001 a prosecutor in Ciudad del Este named Basilisa Vázquez Román investigated a US$100 million transfer from two Ciudad del Este bank branches to Lebanon. Vázquez Román told Brazilian media that 10 Lebanese citizens who own businesses in Ciudad del Este but live in Foz do Iguaçu sent the money through banks in Miami and New York to Lebanese banks.[119]

In addition to activities such as money laundering and drug trafficking, Barakat collected money for Hizballah by selling huge quantities of pirated software smuggled into the TBA from Hong Kong. At the end of 2001, Paraguayan agents confiscated, in the Chaco (a semi-arid region of Bolivia and Paraguay), a shipment of 5,000 pirated Nintendo CDs valued at US$160,000. The seizure uncovered a new route for pirated video games used by Barakat: one part of the shipment arrived by sea and another by air in the Chilean port city of Iquique, where Barakat has several businesses. From there, the merchandise was brought by land to the lower Chaco region, and sent to Barakat's shop, Casa Apollo, in Ciudad del Este.[120]

Another raid on October 31, 2002, in Ciudad del Este, found 4,600 falsified CDs and 80 copying machines capable of cloning up to 20,000 CDs per day in a clandestine lab operated by a Lebanese citizen known as "Samir."[121] The lab was located in the same building where Paraguayan authorities arrested Ali Khalil Mehri (see Mehri, Ali Khalil, Appendix) in his apartment in February 2000. Mehri was charged with piracy of computer programs and CDs and with selling millions of dollars of counterfeit software and funneling the proceeds to Hizballah.

---

[118] "Barakat Resorted to Blackmail To Get Money," *Última Hora* [Asunción, an independent, centrist daily, occasionally critical of the government, strongly anti-Oviedo], December 6, 2001, as translated for FBIS, "Report: Media on Efforts to Combat Terrorist Financial Activity in Triborder Area," December 10, 2001 (FBIS Document ID: LAP20011210000096).

[119] *ABC Color*, December 5, 2001, as translated for FBIS, "FBIS Report: Media on Efforts to Combat Terrorist Financial Activity in Triborder Area," December 10, 2001 (FBIS Document ID: LAP20011210000096).

[120] This incident is reported in *ABC Color* [Internet version-www], May 27, 2002, as translated for FBIS, "Paraguay: Authorities Uncover New Route Used by Hizballah Leader Bakarat," May 27, 2002 FBIS Document ID: LAP20020527000062).

[121] The Ciudad del Este Chamber of Commerce [http://www.pamcham.com.py/mem-cde.html] lists Samir Ali Jaber as the owner of Centro de Pioner Import Export, an electronics business located in the Hijazi Shopping. Center [tel: (595) 61 512-321 511-085 502-212; Fax: (595) 512321; e-mail: pioneer@newnet.com.py. However, confirmation that the arrested "Samir" and Samir Ali Jaber are one and the same individual is lacking. Also see "Arab Merchant Sells 'Incinerated' CD's," *Vanguardia* [Ciudad del Este], February 6, 2003, as translated for FBIS, "Highlights From the Tri-Border Press for the Week 3-7 February," February 11, 2003 (FBIS Document ID: LAP20030211000124); and "Allegedly Incinerated CD's Sold in CDE," *Vanguardia* [Ciudad del Este], January 31, 2003, as translated for FBIS, "Tri-Border Press for the Week of 23-31 January," Tri-Border Press Highlights, February 4, 2003 (FBIS Document ID: LAP20030204000134).

Barakat's fund-raising activities even reportedly included complicated swindling schemes together with Ali Hussein Abdallah ("Ali Tawil"). The two would use a new modus operandi in which modest imports of goods from Asia were established over time.[122] Once confidence was gradually gained with the importers, stings were done to the detriment of the wholesale merchants, who were cheated out of containers of merchandise valued at multimillion dollar sums.

TBA-Related Violence Against Local Officials

The governments of the three TBA countries and local TBA officials often emphasize that terrorism is not a problem in the region. For example, during the Third American Conference Against Terrorism, which met in El Salvador on January 22-24, 2003, representatives from Argentina and Brazil emphasized that no terrorist activity or dormant cells had been detected in the TBA.[123] TBA-based Islamic terrorist groups are not known to engage in acts of international terrorism within the TBA, which lacks high-profile targets other than foreign tourists visiting Iguaçu Falls.

However, unidentified groups have been carrying out unclaimed mafia- or Colombian-style attacks against local officials interfering in their fund-raising activities or against business people refusing to pay a "war tax," which is used in financing terrorist operations in various parts of the world. Many businessmen in the TBA reportedly pay what amounts to a war tax to the armed Arab groups in the region.[124] Others pay extortion to mafia groups. A number of businessmen who have refused to pay have been murdered. In one case, Armando Kassen, a Lebanese citizen who was president of the Paraguayan Arab Chamber of Commerce, fled to Beirut after being convicted of murdering a Ciudad del Este businessman, Ussein Mohamed Taiyen, who was president of the Ciudad del Este Chamber of Commerce.[125] On November 2, 2001, Hizballah leaders in the TBA, reportedly concerned not only about losing members and

---

[122] "Barakat Held in Same Prison as "Beira Mar" Drug Smuggler," *ABC Color*, June 24, 2002, as translated by FBIS, "Paraguay Press Highlights," June 24, 2002 (FBIS Document ID: LAP20020624000088).

[123] Horacio Verbitsky, *Pagina/12* [Buenos Aires; Internet version-www], January 26, 2003, as translated for FBIS, "Argentine Bill To Empower Military To Fight Domestic, Foreign Terrorism Viewed," January 26, 2003 (FBIS Document ID: LAP20030126000047).

[124] "Brazil: Report on Islamic Terrorism in Iguazu Triangle," *al-Watan al-'Arabi* [Paris], January 9, 1998, 22–24, as cited by *Estado de São Paulo*.

[125] "Mastermind of Taiyen's Murder Residing in Beirut," *Vanguardia* [Ciudad del Este], November 11, 2002, as translated for FBIS, "Highlights: Brazil - Paraguay Triborder Press 4-15 Nov 02," November 21, 2002 (FBIS Document ID: LAP20021121000006).

influence to al Qaeda, but also about pressure being increasingly applied on them by security forces in the region, issued a *fatwa* authorizing the use of physical violence against traitors or enemies of the jihad.[126]

More recently, on October 21, 2002, local mafia organizations involved with smuggling and piracy activities in the TBA sent a clear message of their power beyond the region to Uruguayan Customs Director Víctor Lissidini.[127] The TBA Mafia made telephone threats to Lissidini before he was shot at in his car by four armed gunmen on two motorcycles, in reprisal for the confiscation of a batch of counterfeit merchandise bound for Ciudad del Este.[128] The constant seizure of pirate merchandise by authorities in Uruguay apparently provoked the attack. Prior to the attack on his car, mafia operating out of Ciudad del Este and involved with smuggling and pirating CDs and possibly financing Islamic terrorist groups made cellular phone threats to Lissidini and his subordinates. The callers specifically demanded that 2 million confiscated blank CDs belonging to the Piscis Import-Export Company located in Ciudad del Este be released.[129] In another example, on February 24, 2003, two men riding a motorcycle in downtown Foz do Iguaçu shot and seriously wounded the president of the Foz do Iguaçu City Council.[130] It was unclear whether the perpetrators were linked to a particular ethnic group.

Clandestine Terrorist Communications in the TBA

There have been open-source indications that the Islamic terrorist network in the TBA has maintained telephone communications with operatives worldwide, including in the United States. The FBI reportedly traced several telephone calls between the United States and at least one of the TBA cities immediately following the September 11, 2001 terrorist attacks. Whether

---

[126] *Útima Hora*, November 5, 2001, as translated for FBIS, "FBIS Report: Media on Efforts to Combat Terrorist Financial Activity in Triborder Area," December 10, 2001 (FBISDocoument ID: LAP20011210000096).

[127] "Ciudad Del Este Linked To Customs Director Attack," Uruguay Radio Parque [Ciudad del Este], November 26, 2002, as translated for FBIS, "Brazil-Paraguay Triborder Press Highlights: November 25–29, 2002, December 3, 2002 (FBIS Document ID: LAP20021203000105).

[128] "Justicia investiga atentado" [Justice Investigates Attack], *El País* [Montevideo], November 21, 2002; and "Atentado a la colombiana contra vehículo de Lissidini" [Colombian-Style Attack Against the Car of Lissidini], *La República en La Red*, November 21, 2002, 12.

[129] "Threats to Lissidini Possibly Linked to Terrorism," *La República* [Montevideo; unofficial newspaper of Uruguay's largest political party, the leftist Broad Front; Internet version-www), November 21, 2002, as translated by FBIS, November 21, 2002 (FBIS Document ID: LAP20021121000104).

[130] "Foz City Council President Shot in Attack," Itapiru Radio "Segunda Entrega de Noticias" newscast [Ciudad del Este], February 24, 2003, as translated for FBIS, "Tri-Border Radio Highlights 24 Feb 03," Radio Parque [Ciudad del Este], February 24, 2003 (FBIS Document ID: LAP20030226000042).

Islamic terrorists in the TBA played any role in the September 11 attacks in the United States is not known. Some al Qaeda operatives in the TBA may have known in advance about the September 11 attacks and discussed the plot in a mosque in Foz do Iguaçu. At least this is the contention of a Moroccan student, Gueddan Abdel Fatah, 27, who was arrested in early September 2001 in Brazil. Fatah maintains that he overheard Islamic extremists discussing the September 11 al Qaeda attacks against New York and Washington at a mosque in Foz do Iguaçu a week before the attacks took place. Brazilian press reports indicate that he contacted an attorney visiting his prison on September 5, 2001, and asked them to "urgently" deliver a letter to Brazilian, U.S., and Israeli authorities to warn them about an impending attack with "two explosions" that could take place in the United States.[131]

In 2001-02, Islamic terrorist groups reportedly were using the TBA as part of a clandestine communications network using a system known as PABX, which is designed to evade eavesdropping on telephone conversations by spy satellites by connecting various telephone networks. Calls from Saudi Arabia to Brazil, or from Brazil to Pakistan, for example, could be made without raising suspicions. In 2000 the Brazilian Police reportedly detected at least six clandestine communication bases near Foz do Iguaçu that were being used for making and receiving telephone calls to and from the Middle East and Afghanistan.[132] Before the September 11 attacks in the United States, Brazilian investigators were suspicious of what was thought to be merely illegal schemes to reduce the price of telephone calls. After September 11, however, suspicions shifted to possible terrorist links because the illegal calls went to countries like Afghanistan, Pakistan, and Lebanon.

Concerned about what it considered to be the action of Islamic extremist cells in the TBA, Brazil's PF began to operate under cover in the region. Within weeks, the PF discovered various clandestine telephone exchanges suspected of links with Islamic extremism.[133] In 2002,

---

[131] John Daly, "The Suspects: The Latin American connection," *Jane's Terrorism & Security Monitor*, October 1, 2001.

[132] Mario Daniel Montoya, "War on Terrorism Reaches Paraguay's Triple Border," *Jane's Intelligence Review* 13, no. 12 (December 2001): 13.

[133] Expedito Filho and Sílvio Ferreira, with Patrícia Cerqueira, "Rede de clandestinidade" [Clandestine Network], OnlineÉpoca Editora Globo], No. 179, October 22, 2001; João Naves de Oliveira, "Central telefônica leva três à prisão em MS" (Telephone Exchange Takes Three to Prison in MS), Estado.com.br, October 12, 2001; and "Árabes teriam financiado centrais telefônicas piratas no PR" (Arabs Had Financed Pirated Telephone Exchanges in PR), Estadao.com.br, terra.com.br, October 11, 2001.

the Brazilian police closed a dozen telephone switching operations in Foz do Iguaçu and in other nearby cities that could have been used to evade U.S. satellites monitoring telephone traffic.[134]

While living in Foz do Iguaçu in 1999-2001, Lebanese businessman Afif Najib Eid contracted operators of the equipment for clandestine telephone switching operations.[135] Eid, who owns an electronic products store in Ciudad del Este, migrated from Lebanon to Foz do Iguaçu in 1989. Phone records indicate that much of the traffic involved countries such as Afghanistan, Pakistan, and Saudi Arabia.[136] In late 2001, police in Foz do Iguaçu arrested at least one of the clandestine operators, a Lebanese named Muhamed Hassan Atwi and a Brazilian named Paulo César Caramori. Atwi was suspected of operating the illegal telephone services in Paraná State and another in Rio de Janeiro. In the apartment used by the two men, police found a computer and false passports (see Hassan, El Hadi Haha Mohamad).[137]

TBA-Linked Islamic Terrorist Activities Elsewhere in the Southern Cone

The TBA's Islamic extremist and organized crime networks cannot be examined in isolation because they are linked to wider networks in the Latin American region and the world in general. Moreover, Islamic extremists who had been based in the TBA have been spreading out and establishing new support networks, apparently in places also popular with organized crime groups. In late 2002, unidentified TBA intelligence officials commented about two trends regarding the movements of Islamic extremists who had been based in the TBA.[138] It was noted that these extremists were dispersing to smaller towns within the region. For example, they had been seen in towns such Uruguaiana, a Brazilian town on the border with Argentina south of Ciudad del Este; Cascavel in Brazil's Ceará State; and Pedro Juan Caballero in Paraguay, renowned for its potent marijuana crops and scarcity of police.[139] The TBA's Islamic extremists, like mafia members and corrupt officials, also are being attracted to the money-laundering centers along the 1,290-kilometer-long Brazil-Paraguay border. These include, in Brazil, Ponta

---

[134] Larry Rohter, "South America Region Under Watch for Signs of Terrorists," *New York Times*, December 15, 2002, 1A, 32.
[135] "O terror por aqui" (The terror at Home), OnLine Epoca, O Globo.com, No. 179, October 22, 2001.
[136] Larry Rohter, "South America Region Under Watch for Signs of Terrorists," *New York Times*, December 15, 2002, 1A, 32.
[137] Rohter, *New York Times*.
[138] Larry Rohter, "South America Region Under Watch for Signs of Terrorists," *New York Times*, December 15, 2002, 1A, 32.
[139] Rohter, New York Times.

Porã and Coronel Sapucaia in Mato Grosso do Sul State, as well as Cascavel; and, in Paraguay, Pedro Juan Caballero and Capitán Bado.[140]

Intelligence officials also noted that Islamic extremists were branching out into nearby countries with established Arab or Muslim communities, such as Iquique, Chile; Guayaquil, Ecuador; and Maracaibo, Venezuela. There are also indications that Islamic extremists are also moving to São Paulo. As a result of increased security measures implemented in the TBA in the 1999-2002 period, a so-called "second tri-border area" was reportedly developing in the region between Brazil, Bolivia, and Peru.[141]

Chuy, Uruguay, and Chuí, Brazil

A month after the bomb attack against the AMIA building in Buenos Aires in July 1994, Brazilian government suspicion began focusing on the city of Chuí in the southern part of Brazil, at the border with Uruguay. Chuí is the other half of Chuy, which is on the Uruguayan side. It is easy to reach Buenos Aires from Chuí by sea, thereby avoiding border controls. The city has a total of about 1,500 Arab residents.

In about 1994, a Hizballah network reportedly was initially detected using the Chuí zone as a point of distribution of military weapons such as M-16 and AR-15, grenades, and rocket launchers.[142] These groups undoubtedly are linked to those in the TBA. More recently, in 2001, Uruguayan investigations uncovered a cocaine trafficking operation in Chuy that was linked to

---

[140] Clarinha Glock, "Brazil-Paraguay: A Full Plate for Journalists," July 19, 2001, Inter American Press Association [http://www.impunidad.com/atrisk/brasil_paraguay7_19_01E.html], citing PF (Federal Police) reports; and Pedro Oviedo, "En la Triple Frontera se lavan doce mil millones de dólares al año del narcotráfico, según un informe official" [In the Triple Border US$12 billion Is Laundered Per Year From Narcotics Trafficking, According to An Official Report], www.MisionesOnLine.net, no. 745, July 8, 2001, http://misionesonline.net/paginas/action.lasso?-database=noticias3&-layout=web&-response=noticia.html&id=11349&autorizado=si&-search, citing Dr. Guido Rauber *Lavado de Dinero: Triple Frontera—Work Paper Nº 1*, Prevención de Adicciones y Control de Drogas [Subsecretary of Drug Control and Prevention of Addictions], Ministry of Public Health of Misiones Province, Argentina, updated version of December 31, 2000 (original date, August 2, 1999).
[141] Marcio Aith, *Folha de São Paulo* [São Paulo; Internet version-www], November 8, 2002, as translated for FBIS, "Argentine Intelligence Chief Says Terrorism Seeking New 'Tri-border' Area," November 8, 2002 (FBIS Document ID: LAP20021108000025), citing Miguel Angel Toma, chief of Argentina's Secretariat for State Intelligence (Secretaría de Información del Estado—SIDE), in response to a telephone interview question.
[142] Brazilian Officials Warn Uruguay About Islamic Groups at Border," September 1, 1994, 16 (JPRS-TOT-94-036-L).

the Arab and Lebanese Mafias. A Brazilian Federal Police document reportedly states that, "The money obtained from the sale of the product would be used to finance international terrorism."[143]

The Chuí connection to the TBA came into clearer focus in 2001, when a Lebanese named Al-Sa'id Ali Hasan Mukhlis (also spelled Mokhles) was identified as having contacts with Saudi Arabian members of a group of Osama bin Laden militants in the TBA (see Mukhlis, El Sa'id Hassan Ali Mohamed (al-Gama'a al-Islamiyya), Appendix). The mayor of the Brazilian border town of Chuí, Mohammed Kasim (also spelled Kassem) Jomaa ("Mohamed Yoma"), allegedly helped al Said Hassan Hussein Mukhlis' family after Mukhlis was arrested in Chuí on February 27, 1999, following a call by the CIA to detain him on charges of having participated in the Luxor terrorist attack.[144] Mayor Jomaa has been described as the presumed chief of the emerging "Arab Mafia," an organization involved in arms and drug trafficking, money laundering, and exploitation of undocumented workers.[145]

Iquique, Chile

Islamic terrorist ties are believed to exist between the TBA and Iquique in Chile.[146] Iquique is an attractive location for Islamic money launderers and smugglers operating in the TBA. The attraction is partly explained by the fact that Chile has become the fastest-growing hub in South America after Brazil for international narcotics transshipments and money-laundering enterprises.[147] In addition, as pressure from security authorities has increased in the TBA, a number of Islamic militants reportedly have moved to Iquique.

On November 8, 2001, the Chilean government confirmed that it was investigating an alleged Arab financial network with terrorist links that may be engaging in money laundering in Iquique, Chile.[148] It involved Assad Ahmad Barakat and his fellow countryman Kalil Saleh, who

---

[143] Sérgo Gobetti, "PF investiga ligação de prefeito con Bin Laden" (PF Investigates Mayor's Links with bin Laden"), Oestadao.com.br, September 12, 2001.

[144] John Daly, "The Suspects: The Latin American connection," *Jane's Terrorism & Security Monitor*, October 1, 2001.

[145] Enrique Medeot, "El alcalde brasileño que jura no ser amigo de Bin Laden" (The Brazilian Mayor Who Swears That He Isn't A Friend of bin Laden), Clarín.com, September 16, 2001; and *New York Times*, September 27, 2001

[146]Fernando Tejeda and Javier Méndez, "Nexo entre la Triple Frontera e Iquique" [Nexus between the Triple Frontier and Iquique], *El Mercurio* [Santiago], October 13, 2001, http://www.emol.com/noticias/detalle/detalle_diario.asp?idnoticia=0113102001001A0050001.

[147] "New Drug Gangs Spreading in Colombia," *The Global Intelligence Report* (Stratfor), April 3, 2002, citing *El Tiempo*.

[148] *Estrategía* [a Santiago financial daily, Internet version-www], November 9, 2001, as translated for FBIS, "Chile Confirms Alleged Terrorist-Linked Financial Network Under Investigation," November 9, 2001 (FBIS Document

established two import and export firms in Iquique in early June 2001. Investigators confirmed that the money allegedly laundered in Iquique came from Ciudad del Este, and that Barakat's businesses were being used as fronts. The amount laundered was estimated to be several million dollars.

OTHER ORGANIZED CRIME ACTIVITIES IN THE TBA

As suggested in the earlier discussion of TBA-related violence against local officials, Islamic terrorist group activities in the TBA and organized crime activities in the region often cannot be distinguished clearly. In the case of Hizballah, for example, the distinction between Hizballah and the Lebanese Mafia is not at all clear based on the limited amount of material covered in this study. If Hizballah and the Lebanese Mafia are not interconnected, then they probably at least cooperate closely. In addition to unclaimed acts of occasional violence against business people and local officials, the Islamic terrorist groups and organized crime groups in the region engage in illicit activities such as drug and arms trafficking, money laundering, and product piracy. Instead of always pursuing these activities separately, however, the Islamic terrorist groups and organized crime groups in the TBA may collaborate whenever collaboration better serves their mutual interests. Examples of this reported collaboration in the TBA include Hizballah's ties with groups such as the Hong Kong Mafia and the Argentine "Local Connection," al Qaeda's ties with the Chechen and Chinese mafias, and the Egyptian al-Gama'a al-Islamiyya's ties with the Chinese Mafia.

In addition to Islamic terrorist groups and organized crime groups, a third type of group is found in the TBA: corrupt government or security force officials. Corruption at all levels of

---

ID: LAP20011109000089); "Chilean Police Investigate Terrorist Financial Network," *Santiago Times*, January 8, 2002; and Héctor Rojas and Pablo Vergara, *La Tercera de la Hora* [Santiago; a conservative, pro-business, top-circulation daily, Internet version-www], November 8, 2001, as translated for FBIS, "Chilian Police Examine Link to Alleged Triborder Hizballah Financial Network," November 8, 2001 (FBIS Document ID: LAP20011108000085).

government allows the Islamic terrorist and organized crime groups to operate in the TBA and elsewhere in the TBA countries with considerable impunity (see TBA-Related Governmental Corruption).

Indigenous Organized Crime Groups

Argentina

Organized crime in Argentina reportedly is in an incipient stage and is regional rather than international in scope, thriving on the socioeconomic and political conditions prevalent in the country.[149] Furthermore, the only form of organized crime in Argentina that is linked to international cartels is said to be drug trafficking, although the narcotraffickers also traffic in children and women; smuggle and market stolen cars; and engage in tax evasion, embezzlement, fraud, insider trading, and financial swindles.[150] The TBA is of particular concern to the Argentine government in this regard because it serves as a gateway for organized crime to migrate south into the rest of the country.

The Islamic fundamentalists in the TBA reportedly are closely linked to a growing mafia in Argentina that provided important assistance in the 1992 bombing of the Israeli Embassy in Buenos Aires and the 1994 bombing of a Jewish community center (AMIA) in that capital. As the economic and political crisis in Argentina continued in 2002, a criminal group known as "Local Connection," made up of corrupt politicians and former members of the military regime, was reportedly prospering.[151] As a result of its unique organizational relationship between common criminals and public figures, the Local Connection, unlike other Argentine gangs, has enjoyed impunity. It reportedly controls much of what are now major industries in Argentina, including arms and drug trafficking, kidnappings, and Argentina's flourishing industry of dismantling stolen cars for spare parts. The Local Connection is organized like the Italian Mafia in small units, or families, linked to a boss, generally a corrupt police official or someone who served in the military regime. Its members are linked to the fundamentalist Islamic movements

---

[149] Hugo Antolin Almiron, "Organized Crime: A Perspective from Argentina." Chapter 14 in Jay S. Albanese, Dilip K. Das, and Arvind Verma, eds., *Organized Crime: World Perspectives* (Upper Saddle River, New Jersey: Prentice Hall, 2003), 320.

[150] Almiron, 329.

[151] This paragraph is based entirely on Carlos Wagner, special envoy in Buenos Aires, Zero Hora [Porto Alegre], November 10, 2002, as translated by FBIS, "Brazil: Argentine Crime Group "Local Connection" Said To Have Ties to Terrorists in Tri-Border," November 10, 2002 (FBIS Document ID: LAP20021111000047).

that are active in the TBA. The Connection bosses use code names when contacting the fundamentalists in Foz de Iguaçu and Ciudad del Este.

In late 2001, a change of strategy in arms trafficking reportedly took place amid the political and economic crisis that overtook Argentina.[152] Until then, the Local Connection was involved only in big arms deals, such as providing military equipment to groups fighting civil wars, but in late 2001 it began to sell contraband. Since then, Argentina reportedly has been taking the place of Paraguay in smuggling weapons into Brazil, even arms used exclusively by the Argentine armed forces.

Paraguay

Families that began smuggling activities in the TBA, particularly the Morel family, have developed ties with international mafias and have acquired increasing political power and influence in other regions of Paraguay. The Morel clan began a war with the organization of Luiz Fernando da Costa ("Fernandinho Beira-Mar"), when he moved into the Paraguayan border region with Brazil after escaping from prison in March 1997. The two Morel brothers were killed in January 2001, and the clan's patriarch was killed in a Brazilian jail a week later, reportedly at the orders of Beira Mar.[153] The Paraguayan drug families have branched out into lucrative activities such as arms trafficking, mainly to supply organized crime groups in Brazilian cities. Elvio Ramón Cantero Aguero, based in Pedro Juan Caballero, heads one criminal organization operating in the Ciudad del Este area.[154]

Brazilian and U.S. officials generally consider former General Lino César Oviedo to be head of the so-called Paraguay Cartel. He reportedly has amassed at least US$1 billion, including numerous properties in the TBA.[155] At the time of his arrest in June 2000, Oviedo was using Foz do Iguaçu and Ciudad del Este as a base of operations for laundering money.

---

[152] Wagner, "Local Connection."

[153] Mike Ceaser, "Libre comercio de drogas" [Free Trade of Drugs], Noticiasaliadas.org, November 15, 2002, http://www.lapress.org/Summ.asp?lanCode=2&couCode=19.

[154] "Tri-Border Press Highlights," December 2-6, 2002, as translated for FBIS, December 12, 2002 (FBIS Document ID: LAP20021212000099); Cesar Palacios and Oscar Florentín, *Noticias* [Asunción], December 6, 2002, as translated for FBIS, "Paraguay: Police Confiscate Arsenal from Gangster's Home," December 6, 2002 (FBIS Document ID: LAP20021206000030).

[155] This paragraph is based entirely on "El Caso Lino Oviedo y su conexión con la Argentina" [The Lino Oviedo Case and Its Connection with Argentina], *Página12* [Buenos Aires], 2001, citing an Argentine Chamber of Deputies report on money laundering, http://www.pagina12.com.ar/2001/suple/carrio/cap11.pdf.

Non-Indigenous Organized Crime Groups

Crime syndicates from China, Colombia, Corsica, Ghana, Italy, Ivory Coast, Japan, Korea, Lebanon (see Islamic Terrorist Group Activities in the TBA), Mexico, Nigeria, Russia, and Taiwan are known to have operated in the TBA. A number of these groups are reportedly associated with corrupt Paraguayan business executives, politicians, and military officers tied to the ruling Colorado Party.[156] They even reportedly control some news media directors.[157] The influence in the TBA of non-indigenous organized crime networks reportedly is strengthening. These groups are active in Paraguay and along the drug-trafficking route from Colombia to the United States and Europe. Most of these clandestine operations reportedly take place in Ciudad del Este, which is considered a regional center for drug trafficking and arms smuggling. The transactions mostly involve bartering drugs for weapons from Colombian armed rebel groups.[158]

The Colombian, Italian, and Nigerian mafias have been singled out as the main transnational mafias operating in Brazil, but without headquarters in that country.[159] Brazil's Federal Police reported in late 1999 that the Nigerian Mafia operates in various Brazilian cities, including Foz do Iguaçu.[160] According to Uruguayan authorities, these and other principal organized crime groups, including the Japanese *yazuka* (the Japanese word for gangsters) all have a presence in Ciudad del Este, where they have an established criminal structure that is linked to international terrorism.[161] However, if the Italian and Nigerian mafias are active in the TBA there does not appear to be much news media reporting on their activities in the region.

The Chinese

The cultural and social demographics of Ciudad del Este make it an ideal city for the operations of Chinese-speaking criminal groups. In the 1990s, Chinese mafias such as Fuk

---

[156] Jack Sweeney, "DEA Boosts Its Role in Paraguay," *Washington Times*, August 21, 2001.

[157] "Dicen que directores de medios están vinculados con la mafia" [Some Media Directors Are Said To Be Linked to the Mafia], *ABC Color* [Paraguay], April 3, 2002, http://www.una.py/sitios/abc.

[158] Riyadh Alam-al-Din, "Washington Begins the War on Hizballah in the Border Triangle," *Al-Watan al-Arabi* [Paris], December 21, 2001, 18–19, as translated for FBIS, "Report Says US Antiterror Campaign To Target Hizballah Network in S. America" (FBIS Document ID: GMP20011221000179).

[159] Ruy Gomes Silva, Effective Measures to Combat Transnational Organized Crime in Criminal Justice Processes, December 2001, 165.

[160] *O Estado de Sao Paulo* [Internet version], November 23, 1999, as translated by FBIS, "Federal Police Links Local Companies With Nigerian Mafia," November 23, 1999 (FBIS Document ID: FTS19991123001608).

[161] "Ciudad del Este: Centro internacional de mafias, a una hora de vuelo de Uruguay" [Ciudad del Este: International Mafia Center, A One-Hour Flight from Uruguay], La Onda Digital, September 25, 2001, http://www.uruguay.com/laonda/LaOnda/Entrevistas/Diputado%20Alberto%20Scavarelli.htm.

Ching, Big Circle Boys, Flying Dragons, and Tai Chen, mostly from mainland China, established a presence in Ciudad del Este in order to profit from the city's Asian imports.[162] They are considered by authorities to be especially dangerous because they are young groups that do not follow traditional rules, such as staying in their own world and not bothering authorities or diplomats.[163]

Some of these Chinese mafias are called Triads; they specialize in providing "protection" to local Chinese business people and in imposing "taxes" on the containers imported by the Chinese businesses from Asia. When the mafia directly imports goods from Asia, the Chinese business community is obligated to purchase that merchandise, or suffer the consequences of not doing so.[164] As of 2000, at least six Chinese Triads existed in the TBA and were vying for the 7,000 Chinese businesses in Ciudad del Este, from whom they collect up to US$30,000 a month by exporting "protection" money.[165] These groups reportedly originated in Hong Kong, Mainland China, and Taiwan.[166]

These groups can be summarized as follows:

❖ The members of the "Fuk Ching" (also spelled "Fuchien" or "Fu Chin") Triad came from China during the Stroessner regime.[167] They are headed by A. Sahi o Sain ("Mayo") or Feng Cheng Cui. In 2000 this was the most powerful group and consisted of 30 assassins of between 20 and 30 years of age, who also were operating in Foz do Iguaçu.[168] Fuk Ching monopolizes the umbrella market in the TBA.[169]

❖ "Pac Lun Fu" dominates electronics contraband and athletic items in the TBA. It is supported by Brazilian and Paraguayan delinquents who specialize in extorting "protection" money. Anyone who refuses to pay is likely to be murdered.

---

[162] Rotella.

[163] Rotella.

[164] Bartolomé, 7, citing XIV Seminario de Fronteras: Los Desafíos a la Seguridad y Delitos del Siglo XXI, Escuela Superior de Gendarmería, Buenos Aires, 1996, 13–16.

[165] Tripartitite Command of the Three Borders, *Base de Datos SER en el 2000* [Regional Strategic Sercurity Database in 2000], http://www.ser2000.org/protect/docs-sobresalientes/triplef.htm.

[166] Rotella, citing Paraguayan police archives.

[167] For background, see James O. Finckenauer, "Chinese Transnational Organized Crime: The Fuk Ching," (undated) National Institute of Justice International, U.S. Department of Justice, http://www.ojp.usdoj.gov/nij/ international/ctoc.html, citing Chin, Ko-lin, *Chinatown Gangs* (Oxford: Oxford University Press, 1996).

[168] Tripartitite Command.

[169] "Taiwanese Mafia Boss Arrested," *Vanguardia* [Ciudad del Este], November 28, 2002, as translated for FBIS, "Brazil-Paraguay Triborder Press Highlights: November 25–29, 2002," December 3, 2002 (FBIS Document ID: LAP20021203000105).

❖ The "Tai Chen Saninh" Group originated in Hong Kong. It has been fighting to displace the other Triads in the TBA.[170] A Tai Chen boss in Ciudad del Este was shot to death in 1998 after attempting to extort US$200,000 from a Taiwanese immigrant building an industrial park in the city.[171]

❖ The "Continental" Group has been seeking to control the wall-clock market in the TBA.

❖ Along with the Chinese Triads and the Japanese *yakuza*, the Big Circle Boys is one of the most prominent types of groups involved in Asian-based transnational crime.[172] Big Circle Boys (Dai Huen Jai, or BCB) is a loosely affiliated group of gangs operating independently and cooperating only when necessary. Although not a Triad, the BCB's operations are considered to be nearly as sophisticated as those of the Triads. BCB members are active in drug trafficking, migrant smuggling and large-scale credit card forgery and fraud. BCB is believed to be working with a variety of transnational crime syndicates, including the Russian/Eastern European Mafia, and outlaw motorcycle gangs.[173]

❖ The Flying Dragons appears to be an affiliate of the same overall organization as New York's Flying Dragons, a vicious Chinese street gang, which is the enforcement sector of the Hip Sing Triad, a Fukienese Triad.[174]

Although the Chinese Mafia in the TBA is characterized by internecine rivalries, it is known to collaborate with the Islamic terrorist groups in the region. At least two organizations—the Sung-I and Ming families—have engaged in illegal operations with the Egyptian al-Gama'a al-Islamiyya.[175] The Sung-I family, which is based in the Paraguayan town of Hernandárias, used three photography and electronic businesses located in Ciudad del Este as fronts for its

---

[170] Tripartitite Command.

[171] Rotella.

[172] Canadian Security Intelligence Service (CSIS), "Transnational Criminal Activity," November 1998, http://www.fas.org/irp/threat/back10e.htm.

[173] For additional information, see Criminal Intelligence Service Canada (CSIS), "Asian-Based Organized Crime," 1998, http://www.cisc.gc.ca/AnnualReport1998/Cisc1998en/asian98.htm.

[174] Amy O'Neill Richard, "International Trafficking in Women to the United States: A Contemporary Manifestation of Slavery and Organized Crime," An Intelligence Monograph of the Director of Central Intelligence (DCI) Exceptional Intelligence Analyst Program, Center for the Study of Intelligence, Central Intelligence Agency, April 2000, U.S. Department of State Web site, http://usinfo.state.gov/topical/global/traffic/report/homepage. htm#contents, based on interview with INS, New York, May 1999.

[175] Bartolomé, 8; and *ABC Color*, February 24, 2003, as translated by FBIS, "Chinese Mafia Linked to Islamic Fundamentalists," in "Paraguay Press Highlights," February 25, 2003 (FBIS Document ID: LAP20030225000094).

activities. In December 2000, Sung-I sold a shipment of munitions to the Islamic Group, sending it to Egypt by ship as "medical equipment." The Cameroon-flagged vessel was intercepted in the Cypriot port of Limasol. The Ming family managed Islamic Group funds from Ciudad del Este in the financial circuit that includes Guyana and the Cayman Islands.[176] An example of collaboration between the Chinese Mafia and Islamic terrorist groups in the TBA is the distribution chain for counterfeit manufacture of mass-market items, such as toys, running from Hong Kong to Hizballah extremists.[177]

The Chinese community in Ciudad del Este has such a dynamic trade in illicit Asian contraband that the Taiwanese Chinatrust Bank established its only Latin American branch in the city.[178] The significance of the Chinese Mafia threat in the TBA appeared to be confirmed by the formal demand made in 2001 by a group of 15 Taiwanese industrialists who are members of Taiwan's Ministry of Economic Affairs. The industrialists conditioned their proposal for establishing their industries in the Eastern Industrial Park of Ciudad del Este on the eradication of the Chinese Mafia in the TBA by local authorities.[179]

Reportedly, the Hong Kong Mafia engages in large-scale trafficking in pirated products from mainland China to Ciudad del Este and maintains strong ties with the pro-Iranian Hizballah in the TBA.[180] Ayrton Nascimiento Vicente, who was chief of Brazil's TBA Command, an organization created by the governments of Argentina, Brazil, and Paraguay to control the zone, confirmed that Chinese and Korean mafias have been identified in the TBA, including in Foz do Iguaçu and Ciudad del Este.[181]

---

[176] Bartolomé, 8, citing Roberto Godoy, "Tríplice Fronteira é vigiada há 20 anos," *O Estado de São Paulo*, November 11, 2001.

[177] *ABC Color* (Internet version-www), November 22, 2002, as translated for FBIS, "Hong Kong Mafia Linked to Hizballah in Tri-Border Region" (FBIS Document ID: LAP20021122000047).

[178] Bartolomé, 7, citing "The Bank in the Future of South America," *Taipei Today* 18, no. 2 (March–April 1999).

[179] Bartolomé, 8, citing "Empresarios taiwaneses piden erradicación de la mafia china," *Noticias*, November 18, 2001.

[180] *ABC Color* [Internet version-www], November 22, 2002, as translated for FBIS, "Paraguay: 'Strong Ties' Seen Between Hong Kong Mafia, Tri-border Based Hizballah," November 22, 2002 (FBIS Document ID: LAP20021122000059).

[181] Bartolomé, 5, citing "Afirman que es imposible la vigilancia en la Triple Frontera" [Affirmation That Vigilance in the Triborder Region Is Impossible], *La Nación* [Buenos Aires], April 2, 2000; and Aloisio Milani, "Máfia chinesa extorque e executa em São Paulo" [Chinese Mafia Extorts and Executes in São Paulo], Jornal-laboratório da Faculdade de Comunicação Social Cásper Líbero, no. 28 (December 2001), http://biondi.fcl.com.br/facasper/jornalismo/esquinas/noticia.cfm?secao=4&codigo=87]

As a result of the Chinese groups' ability to bribe Paraguayan judges, they have been able to operate with impunity, according to the consul general of Taiwan in Ciudad del Este.[182] In 2001 the Paraguayan government made an effort to neutralize the activities of the Chinese mafias, but only minor successes were reported. In July 2001, authorities in Ciudad del Este arrested Chinese citizen Wu Wen Huan, one of the mafia capos in the TBA. Local Chinese business people denounced him for his extortion tactics. Between 1997 and 2000, Wu Wen Huan's company, Floresta SA, had registered more than 600 untaxed imports.[183] And that October, Paraguayan police arrested Cheng Tin Tsang, one of the new Chinese Mafia capos in the TBA, along with two other Asian criminal suspects. The three were residing in Foz do Iguaçu and using North American and European passports to avoid being detained as Asians.[184]

Another alleged chief of Chinese organized crime in the TBA, a young woman named Chia Hui ("Erica") Pai, was arrested in late 2002. According to *ABC Color*, Chia Hui was accused of being the mastermind in the torture and attempted murder of Chinese businessman Guillermo Lin, who survived being shot in the head and thrown into the Río Paraná.[185] Lin later pressed charges and testified against his alleged torturers, among them Shih Soung Mou ("Roberto Shih").[186] People connected to the Chinese Mafia in Ciudad del Este reportedly paid US$12,000 to obtain the release of Chia Hui on bail.[187]

Instead of having their operations disrupted by these occasional arrests, the Chinese Mafia groups appear to be using the TBA as a base for expanding their thriving businesses into Argentina and Brazil. An investigation by Argentina's National Gendarmerie (Gendarmería Nacional), a paramilitary force, found that members of the Chinese mafias enter Argentine

---

[182] Bartolomé, 16, citing "Mafia, amparada por la justicia" [Mafia protected by justice], *ABC Color*, September 28, 2001.

[183] Bartolomé, 7–8, citing "Procesarán por evasion a supuesto capomafioso," *ABC*, September 17, 2001; "Trial Begins for 'Mafia Boss' Chinese Citizen," *ABC Color*, November 29, 2002, as translated for FBIS (FBIS Document ID: LAP20021129000064); and "Taiwanese Mafia Boss Arrested," *Vanguardia* [Ciudad del Este], November 28, 2002, as translated for FBIS, "Brazil-Paraguay Triborder Press Highlights: November 25–29, 2002," December 3, 2002 (FBIS Document ID: LAP20021203000105).

[184] Bartolomé, 8, citing "Detienen a chinos e indagan possible nexo con la mafia," *Noticias*, October 26, 2001.

[185] "Captured Chinese Mafia Boss To Be Freed," *ABC Color*, December 13, 2002, as translated by FBIS, "Highlights: Paraguay Press," December 13, 2002, (FBIS Document ID: LAP20021213000113).

[186] Ibid.

[187] Ibid.

territory with tourist visas issued by the Paraguayan consulates of the TBA's Puerto Iguazú or nearby Eldorado (an Argentine town in the department adjacent to Iguazú Department). The objective of these Chinese criminals is to establish themselves in the duty-free zone of Argentina's San Luis Province.[188]

The Colombians

Although the Colombian drug cartels are known to have been operating in Brazil and Paraguay for years, information on their activities in the TBA is not readily available in news media. In the case of Colombia's principal guerrilla organization, the Revolutionary Armed Forces of Colombia (Fuerzas Armadas Revolucionarias de Colombia—FARC), there appears to be a direct connection between the TBA's function as a drug-trafficking outlet and the FARC. The FARC derives much of its operating funds from drug-related activities and is known to do business with the Brazilian, Colombian, and Russian mafias. Little substantive information on FARC activities in the TBA has been reported in news media, but links between crime syndicates in Ciudad del Este and the FARC reportedly date at least from the mid-1990s, when General Oviedo protected Brazilian drug trafficker Luiz Fernando Da Costa ("Fernandinho Beira Mar"). Da Costa was captured in southern Colombia in April 2001 in the company of FARC rebels.[189]

The FARC's guerrilla elite actually has a haven located not far from the TBA. Of three known FARC havens in Brazil, the biggest of them is located in the small city of Guaíra in the southern part of Brazil's Paraná State at the Paraguay border, only 100 miles (161 kilometers) north of Foz do Iguaçu (see Figure 1, The FARC's Havens in Brazil). It is located on a 6,000-hectare ranch belonging to businessman Ahmad Mohamad, a Lebanese naturalized in Paraguay and arrested by Brazil's Federal Police in September 2002.[190]

---

[188] Bartolomé, 8, citing "Investigan a la mafia china en Misiones," *La Nación* [Buenos Aires], October 24, 1999.
[189] Strafor Global Intelligence Update, "Paraguay Drug Trade and U.S. American Facilities, Personnel at Greater Risk," August 14, 2001, http://www.mapinc.org/drugnews/v01/n1499/a06.html.
[190] Roberto Godoy, "As Farc usam Brasil para abrigar elite da guerrilha" [FARC uses Brazil to shelter the guerrilla elite], *O Estado de São Paulo* [Internet version: Estadao.com.br], March 1, 2003, http://www.estado.estadao.com.br/ editorias/2003/03/01/pol024.html.

The Russians

In about 1996, members of the Russian Mafia reportedly began exploring Paraguay, as they did Colombia, Argentina, and Brazil.[191] Russian Mafia groups reportedly were seeking out contacts with the mafia of countries belonging to the Southern Cone Common Market (Mercosur), principally those operating from the drug-trafficking zones of Pedro Juan Caballero-Ponta Porã and Ciudad del Este-Foz do Iguaçu on the Paraguay-Brazil border. The intention of the Russians reportedly would be to ally themselves with the capos of the South American mafias in order to maximize the distribution of cocaine in Europe. They began by seeking to oust the Brazilian and Nigerian cartels based in border towns such as Pedro Juan Caballero.[192] However, if the Russian Mafia has a growing presence in the region and is working with bin Laden in an attempt to establish an al Qaeda presence in the TBA, as claimed by Judge Walter Fanganiello Maierovitch in 2001, this is not evident from the very limited news media reports on the subject.[193]

According to political scientist Bruce Michael Bagley, the Russian Mafia presence in Argentina, specifically Chechen gangs, has been linked primarily to the use of Argentina as a transit country for Andean cocaine shipments to Europe, arms trafficking to Brazil and Colombia, and money laundering. Bagley notes that Argentine intelligence sources have detected contacts between Chechen separatist groups and Islamic terrorists in the TBA and suspect Chechen use of these networks for arms-smuggling purposes.

---

[191] "Paraguay es uno de los países explorados por mafia rusa" [Paraguay is one of the countries explored by the Russian mafia], *ABC Color*, October 16, 1997.
[192] "Temen que mafia rusa ofrezca armas a cambio de cocaína en la frontera" [Fear that the Russian mafia offers arms in exchange for cocaine at the border], *ABC Color*, November 3, 1997; and Guaracy Mingardi, "Money and the International Drug Trade in São Paulo," *International Social Science Journal*, no. 169 (September 2001): 383.
[193] Germano Oliveira.

TBA-Related Governmental Corruption

Argentina

The convergence of interests among corrupt government officials and members of organized crime and terrorist groups operating in the TBA is illustrated by the revelations in July 2002 made by a witness in the case of the July 1994 bombing of the AMIA in Buenos Aires. The witness, Abdolghassem Mesbahi, a former Iranian intelligence officer, testified to Argentine investigators that the Iranian government organized and carried out the attack and then paid then-president Carlos Saúl Menem US$10 million to cover it up.[194] The charges against Menem have never been substantiated, and he vigorously denies them. However, Menem acknowledged that he has had a bank account in Switzerland since 1986.[195] As president, Menem, whose parents migrated to Argentina from Syria, appointed a Syrian army colonel to be customs overseer at Buenos Aires's Ezeiza International Airport, which has been described as "a major hub for smuggling in South America."[196]

Brazil

A 1,198-page report by the Drug Traffic Investigating Commission of Brazil's Congress released in November 2000 accuses 827 individuals—including two federal deputies (congressmen), two former state governors, 15 state deputies, and scores of mayors, judges, police officers, lawyers, and even officials from the neighboring countries of Bolivia, Paraguay, and Suriname—of organized crimes ranging from drug trafficking to arms trafficking to tax evasion.[197] The report concluded that drug-related corruption is so widespread that it is impossible to clean up in the short term without calling in the military and restructuring and rearming the country's police. Another Brazilian congressional report released in mid-2002 on

---

[194] "Slow-Motion Justice in Argentina," *New York Times*, March 11, 2003, A24; and Larry Rohter, "Iran Blew Up Jewish Center In Argentina, Defector Says," *New York Times*, July 22 2002, A1, A6.

[195] Larry Rohter, "World Briefing Americas: Menem Acknowledges Swiss Account," *New York Times*, July 25, 2002, 9.

[196] Martin Edwin Andersen, "Al-Qaeda Across the Americas," *Insight on the News* 17, no. 44 (November 26, 2001): 20–21.

[197] Andrew Downie, "Corruption's Roots Deep and Wide-reaching in Brazil," *Christian Science Monitor*, December 14, 2000; "Investigation Shows Pervasive Impact of Drug Trade in Brazil," *America's Insider* 1, no. 9 (December 8, 2000): 6.

the nationwide surge in highway robberies of truck cargo called for the indictment of 100 politicians, police, and entrepreneurs allegedly involved in the theft of cargo[198] As a money-laundering center, Foz do Iguaçu plays an important role in this widespread corruption (see Money Laundering, Foz do Iguaçu).

Mato Grosso mafia figure João Arcanjo Ribeiro, with US$50 million in Swiss banks and a hotel in Miami valued at US$50 million, was sought by the PF and Interpol in more than 100 countries on charges of heading a ring linked to arms trafficking and diamonds, money laundering, and a series of assassinations.[199] He has also been linked to the TBA-based CC-5 accounts scheme and to money-launderer Alberto Yussef.[200] Arcanjo Ribeiro was captured in Montevideo, Uruguay, in early April 2003, and subsequently was seeking to avoid extradition to Brazil.

Paraguay

Corruption, an old tradition in Paraguay, has reached all the way up to the presidency. The former regime of Alfredo Stroessner was reportedly involved in drug trafficking.[201] More recently, President Raúl Cubas was forced to resign as a result of a drug-related scandal. It was widely believed in Paraguay that Cubas had a hand in the assassination of his political rival, Vice President Luis María Argãna, who was gunned down on the streets of the capital, Asunción, on March 23, 1999, by hired assassins in camouflage gear.[202] In October 2000, José Tomas

---

[198] Raymond Colitt, "Brazil Tracks Down the Real Culprits Behind Surge in Highway Robberies," *Financial Times* [London], May 2, 2002, 10.

[199] Source: *Istoé* OnLine, no. 1740 (February 5, 2003).

[200] Amaury Ribeiro Jr. e Sônia Filgueiras – Foz do Iguaçu (PR), "Ralo da impunidade" [Used-Up Impunity], *Istoé* OnLine, February 2, 2003.

[201] See, for example, Kai Bird and Max Holland, "Paraguay: the Stroessner Connection," *The Nation* 241 (tober 26, 1985), 401.

[202]Tim McGirk, "Assassination!," *Time International* 153, no. 13 (April 5, 1999): 34, http://www.time.com/time/magazine/intl/article/0,9171,1107990405-23175,00.html; "Paraguai: Estava no Brasil: General Oviedo é preso em Foz do Iguaçu" [Paraguay: He was in Brazil: General Oviedo Is Captured in Foz do Iguaçu], *Veja*, no. 1,654 (June 21, 2000), http://veja.abril.com.br/210600/p_055a.html; "Paraguay Vice-President's Killers Jailed," BBC News, October 25, 2000, http://news.bbc.co.uk/1/hi/world/americas/989401.stm; "Brasil amenaza extraditar a Lino

Centurion was sentenced to seven years in prison for corruption during his tenure as chief of the counternarcotics secretariat.[203]

Governmental, political, and diplomatic corruption in Paraguay and the TBA allows individuals associated with organized crime and terrorist groups to bribe judges, purchase entry visas, and engage in any number of other criminal activities that might overlap with legitimate economic activities. An investigation conducted by Paraguayan authorities found that an average of 570 foreigners annually enter the country through the Ciudad del Este Airport using irregular documents, after paying bribes averaging US$5,000.[204]

Reports of this criminal enterprise began surfacing in mid-1998, when Squadron 51 of Argentina's National Gendarmerie (Gendarmería Nacional) detained a Paraguayan woman in Chaco Province in possession of 13 false passports (seven Lebanese and six South Korean). She was also carrying an official Paraguayan "This visa was issued by judicial order" seal and visas applications.[205] Argentine and Paraguayan authorities determined that the interim Paraguayan consul in Salta, Juana Maidana de Villagra, belonged to an illicit group specializing in illegal documents. In six months, this consul issued more than 500 illegal visas, collecting US$900 for each.[206] She received a two-year prison sentence.

In early November 2001, Paraguay's judge Carlos Cálcena charged that some of Paraguay's consulates had been converted into veritable offices for falsifying documents.[207] That year, the Directorate of Legal Affairs in Paraguay's Ministry of Foreign Affairs also identified as "vulnerable" the consulates in Santa Cruz, Bolivia; Salta, Eldorado, and Buenos Aires, Argentina; Iquique, Chile; and São Paulo, Foz do Iguaçu, Ponta Porã, and Curitiba, Brazil.[208]

Oviedo" [Brazil Threatens to Extradite Lino Oviedo], *Clarín* [Buenos Aires], July 16, 2002, http://www.clarin.com/ ultimo_momento/notas/2002/07/16/m-416641.htm; and "Oviedo Denies Ties To Brazilian Drug Smuggler," *Avance* [Ciudad del Este; Internet version-www], June 26, 2002, as translated for FBIS, "Paraguay Press Highlights," June 26, 2002 (FBIS Document ID: LAP20020626000113).

[203] "Paraguay: Political Rights and Civil Liberties," *Freedom in the World, 2001–2002*, Freedom House, 2002, http://freedomhouse.org/research/freeworld/2002/countryratings/paraguay2.htm.

[204] Bartolomé, 18, citing "Comando terroristas se refugian en la Triple Frontera" [Terrorist commandos seek haven in theTriborder Area], *El País*, November 9, 2001.

[205] Bartolomé, 17, citing "Apresan con pasaportes a una mujer" [Woman apprehended with passports], *La Nación* [Buenos Aires], June 24, 1998; and "Investigan si hay una red que tramita pasaportes a libaneses" [Existence of a network trafficking in Lebanese passports being investigated], *La Nación*, June 25, 1998.

[206] Bartolomé, 17, "Ordenan la captura de otros 17 árabes" [Another 17 Arabs ordered captured], *Noticias*, September 27, 2001.

[207] Bartolomé, 17–18, citing "Comandos terroristas se refugian en la Triple Frontera" [Terrorist commandos find safehaven in Triborder Area], *El País*, November 9, 2001.

[208] Bartolomé, 18, citing "La frontera es el punto clave" [The border is the key point], *Noticias*, October 7, 2001.

Post-September 11, 2001 investigations carried out in the TBA found that numerous Lebanese citizens residing in Ciudad del Este had entered Paraguay with illicit visas. The most well-known case was that of Assad Ahmad Barakat, who was able to enter Paraguay in 1989 using a visa obtained from the Paraguayan Consulate in Panama, which was not authorized to issue visas.[209] Until he was arrested and recalled on September 26, 2001, the Paraguayan consul in Miami, Carlos Weiss, had allegedly sold more than 300 passports, visas, and shipping documents to individuals heading to the TBA since June 1999. His customers for visas or passports included about 20 Lebanese, three of whom were on the FBI terrorist watch list, but who had never been in the United States, and terrorist suspects from Egypt and Syria, all of whom were planning to move to Ciudad del Este.[210]

Money Laundering

TBA in General

Although the extent of narcotics trafficking in the TBA is unclear, criminal elements in Ciudad del Este and Foz do Iguaçu specialize in the laundering of drug money. As of 2000-01, the amount of money being laundered in the TBA reportedly was averaging US$12 billion per year, but estimates of the amount of money laundering in the TBA vary widely and cannot be considered reliable (see Table 1).[211] Foz do Iguaçu appears to be the principal money-laundering center, followed by Ciudad del Este. In any case, the amounts laundered in the TBA probably are in the billions of dollars per year. Until about 2000, the most popular financial mechanism for laundering money in the TBA appeared to be the CC-5 account, which is an account that belongs

---

[209] Bartolomé, 17.

[210] Mendel, citing Bill Rogers, "Arabs Accuse Paraguay Police of Extortion," Voice of America (VOA.com), http://www.voanews.com (accessed October 18, 2001); and Larry Rohter, "Terrorists Are Sought in Latin Smugglers' Haven," *New York Times*, September 27, 2001, http://www.nytimes.com; and Bartolomé, 17, citing "Fiscala imputa a Weiss por la concesión irregular de visas" [Judge reprimands Weiss for the irregular issuance of visas], *ABC Color*, September 27, 2001.

[211] Oviedo, citing Dr. Guido Rauber *Lavado de Dinero: Triple Frontera —Work Paper N° 1*, Prevención de Adicciones y Control de Drogas [Subsecretary of Drug Control and Prevention of Addictions], Ministry of Public Health of Misiones Province, Argentina, updated version of December 31, 2000 (original date, August 2, 1999).

to someone residing outside the country.[212] It is often opened with false identity documents, making investigations difficult (see TBA-Related Governmental Corruption, Brazil). By 2000 the TBA mafiosi—better known as dollar exchangers—reportedly were laundering billions of dollars through new mechanisms that had superceded the CC-5 accounts.[213]

Table 1. Amounts of Money Reported Laundered in the Tri-Border Area (TBA), 1992–2001 (in US dollars)

Period	Amount	TBA Location of Activity
2000–2001	$12 billion per year[214]	TBA in general
2000	$25 billion[215]	TBA in general
2000	$5 billion annual average[216]	Ciudad del Este
1998–99	$12 billion total[217]	Foz do Iguaçu
1996–97	$18 billion total[218]	Foz do Iguaçu
1992–98	$70 billion total[219]	Foz do Iguaçu
1992–98	$30 billion total[220]	Foz do Iguaçu

---

[212] The CC-5 account is a special account created by the Central Bank of Brazil, supposedly for foreigners, in order to allow Paraguayan money to be more cheaply and quickly converted to dollars and deposited on the same day in local Brazilian banks.

[213] Pedro Pablo Peñaloza, "Brasil prepara 'el mayor juicio del mundo'" [Brazil Prepares the World's Greatest Trial], talcualdigital.com, *ABC Color*, August 8, 2001, http://www.talcualdigital.com/ediciones/2001/08/08/p22s2.htm.

[214] Pedro Oviedo, "En la Triple Frontera se lavan doce mil millones de dólares al año del narcotráfico, según un informe official" [In the Triple Border US$12 billion Is Laundered Per Year From Narcotics Trafficking, According to An Official Report], www.MisionesOnLine.net, no. 745, July 8, 2001, http://misionesonline.net/paginas/action.lasso?-database=noticias3&-layout=web&-response=noticia.html&id=11349&autorizado=si&-search, citing Dr. Guido Rauber *Lavado de Dinero: Triple Frontera —Work Paper N° 1*, Prevención de Adicciones y Control de Drogas [Subsecretary of Drug Control and Prevention of Addictions], Ministry of Public Health of Misiones Province, Argentina, updated version of December 31, 2000 (original date, August 2, 1999).

[215] Pedro Pablo Peñaloza, "Brasil prepara 'el mayor juicio del mundo'" [Brazil Prepares the World's Greatest Trial], talcualdigital.com, *ABC Color*, August 8, 2001, http://www.talcualdigital.com/ediciones/2001/08/08/p22s2.htm.

[216] "Paraguay: Lack of Control System on Border with Brazil Allows Currency Flight," BBC Monitoring Americas – Political [London], January 23, 2003, 1, citing *ABC Color* Web site, January 22, 2003.

[217] Policarpo Junior, "Tem famosos no meio: Polícia apura um bilionário esquema de remessa ilegal de dinheiro ao exterior e já tem nomes de gente graúda" [They Have Famous People Among Them: Police Expedite a Billion-Real Scheme for Remitting Illegal Money Abroad and Already Have the Names of Big-Shots], *Veja on-line*, no. 1,755 (June 12, 2002), http://veja.abril.com.br/120602/p_046.html.

[218] Amaury Ribeiro Jr. and Sonia Filgueiras, "Sieve of Impunity," *Istoé* [Internet version-www], February 5, 2003, as translated for FBIS, "Brazil: Federal Police, FBI Unveil $30 Billion Money Laundering Scheme," February 5, 2003 (FBIS Document ID: LAP20030203000075).

[219] This paragraph is based entirely on Oviedo, citing Dr. Guido Rauber *Lavado de Dinero: Triple Frontera —Work Paper N° 1*, Prevención de Adicciones y Control de Drogas [Subsecretary of Drug Control and Prevention of Addictions], Ministry of Public Health of Misiones Province, Argentina, updated version of December 31, 2000 (original date, August 2, 1999).

[220] Marcelo Aguiar, with Mauri König, "Cascata de Dólares" [Cascade of Dollars], *Dinheiro* na Web [SãoPaulo], April 6, 2001, http://www.terra.com.br/dinheironaweb/189/financas/189_cascata_dolares.htm.

[220] "Quadrilha lava R$ 30 bilhões em dois anos" [Gang Launders 30 Billion Reais in Two Years], *Correiro Braziliense* [Brasília], November 16, 2000, http://www2.correioweb.com.br/cw/2000-11-16/mat_17077.htm.

In comparison with Ciudad del Este and Foz do Iguaçu, Puerto Iguazú is not known as a major money-laundering center. Instead, the third most important money-laundering center in the TBA appears to be the popular tourist destination known as Iguaçu Falls, which has many foreign exchange bureaus. After receiving large deposits from various parts of Brazil, the exchange shops of Iguaçu Falls forward the money to nonresident CC-5 accounts in Paraguay. In mid-2001, Brazil's Public Prosecutor's Office, specifically the Organized Crime and Special Investigation Division of the Federal Police (Polícia Federal—PF), was investigating 212 cases involving capital flight from Iguaçu Falls totaling more than US$100 million.[221]

Ciudad del Este

In the assessment of the U.S. Department of State, Paraguay is a principal money-laundering center. Money laundering in the country is facilitated by the fact that the multi-billion dollar contraband re-export trade is centered in Ciudad del Este, which is outside the government's regulatory scope.[222] There are no controls on the amount of currency that can be brought into or out of the country, and there are no cross-border reporting requirements. Little in the way of personal background information is required to open a bank account or to make financial transactions in Paraguay; therefore, there is a high incidence of money-laundering activities. Narcotics trafficking generates an estimated 40 percent of money laundering in Paraguay.

Carlos Altemburger, chief of Paraguay's antiterrorist unit, acknowledged in September 2002 that terrorists use the TBA to finance their operations by remitting large amounts of dollars from Ciudad del Este to the Middle East.[223] A minimum of US$5 billion, equivalent to 50 percent of Paraguay's gross domestic product, is reportedly laundered annually in Paraguay, practically all of it in Ciudad del Este.[224] Money laundering is facilitated in Ciudad del Este by the existence of more than 20 illegal foreign-exchange shops (Casas de Cambio, which are

---

[221] Clarinha Glock, "Brazil-Paraguay: A Full Plate for Journalists," Inter American Press Association, July 19, 2001, http://www.impunidad.com/atrisk/brasil_paraguay7_19_01E.html.

[222] This paragraph is based in part on U.S. Department of State, ISCSR-2002.

[223] "Entrevista: tráfico en la "triple frontera" [Interview: Traffic in the "Triple Border], BBCMundo.com, September 3, 2002, http://news.bbc.co.uk/hi/spanish/specials/2001_-_11_de_septiembre_2002/newsid_2234000/2234706.stm.

[224] Oviedo.

concentrated near the Friendship Bridge).[225] At least half of them have no name, other than a sign "foreign exchange." The shops trade only dollars, reais, and guaranies. An estimated 50 percent of all banking transactions registered in Ciudad del Este belong to the category of illicit transactions, in violation of Law 1025.[226] US$3 billion is reportedly laundered annually in Ciudad del Este from five principal sources: contraband, fraud, assaults, tax evasion, and trafficking of drugs and weapons.[227]

Foz do Iguaçu

The exchange-evasion model used by Brazilian money launderers in the TBA consists of making deposits in exchange houses in Foz do Iguaçu, from where they are distributed into CC-5-type accounts in exchange houses in Ciudad del Este.[228] Foz do Iguaçu reportedly had 13 exchange houses in late 2000, after 20 were closed on March 31, 2000, for operating illegally and engaging in laundering activities.

A Foz do Iguaçu prosecutor affirmed in early June 1999 that a mafia operates in Foz do Iguaçu, where 40 percent of the local companies are fronts created only to launder money and to send it abroad.[229] Brazil's PF found that Brazilian industrialist Sílvio Roberto Anspach, one of the biggest money launderers in Brazil's history, centered his money-laundering activities in Foz do Iguaçu.[230]

The TBA and its CC-5 accounts played a central role in a major money-laundering scheme uncovered by Brazilian and U.S. investigators in 2000 and involving many Brazilian

---

[225] "Paraguay: Lack of Control System on Border with Brazil Allows Currency Flight," BBC Monitoring Americas – Political [London], January 23, 2003, 1, citing *ABC Color* Web site, January 22, 2003.
[226] Bartolomé, 9.
[227] Bartolomé, 9, citing Camarasa and a statement made in 2000 by the head of Holland's ABN's bank branch in Ciudad del Este.
[228] Bartolomé, 9.
[229] Mario Osava, "Ciudades de América Latina/Brasil: Lavado y fuga de capitales en la frontera con Paraguay" [Cities of Latin America/Brazil: Laundering and Flight of Capital on the Border with Paraguay], Inter-Press Service, June 6, 1999, http://ips.org/Spanish/mundial/indices/Correo/cor0606051.htm.
[230] "Quadrilha lava," *Correiro Braziliense.*

government officials. In early 2002, a Brazilian police chief and two experts in Foz do Iguaçu money laundering traveled to the United States to investigate the Banestado bank.[231] At the end of the investigation, they had uncovered 135 accounts controlled by 12 Brazilian dealers who between 1996 and 1997 had remitted US$18 billion that were deposited into tax havens by means of 35,000 accounts. In the operation, known as the CC-5 accounts scheme, the investigators learned that the same account holders had sent more than US$12 billion to the same accounts in 1998 and 1999.[232]

One can easily use the CC-5 account to launder money by opening an account in Ciudad del Este in the name of a fictitious person and having the amount transferred back to Brazil. During the 1996-99 period, the scheme mounted by Banestado helped hundreds of politicians, traffickers, and smugglers to send, through the Brazilian dollar dealers, US$30 billion to Switzerland and other tax havens.

The Foz do Iguaçu CC-5 accounts scheme had six steps, as follows:[233]

❖ The individuals who wanted to send money abroad using irregular methods opened contact with a group of 12 money exchangers in Foz do Iguaçu;

❖ The 12 money exchangers, all of whom own exchange houses based in Paraguay, opened accounts in five banks in Foz do Iguaçu, depositing a total of 12 billion reais. The accounts were opened using about 2,000 phony names.

❖ From the five banks in Foz do Iguaçu, the money was remitted abroad through CC-5 accounts;

❖ In the Banestado branch in New York, the money was deposited in 137 accounts, all in the name of companies registered in off-shore havens;

---

[231] Amaury Ribeiro Jr. and Sonia Filgueiras, "Sieve of Impunity," *Istoé* [Internet version-www], February 5, 2003, as translated for FBIS, "Brazil: Federal Police, FBI Unveil $30 Billion Money Laundering Scheme," February 5, 2003 (FBIS Document ID: LAP20030203000075).

[232] Policarpo Junior, "Tem famosos no meio: Polícia apura um bilionário esquema de remessa ilegal de dinheiro ao exterior e já tem nomes de gente graúda" [They Have Famous People Among Them: Police Expedite a Billion-Real Scheme for Remitting Illegal Money Abroad and Already Have the Names of Big-Shots], *Veja on-line*, no. 1,755 (June 12, 2002), http://veja.abril.com.br/120602/p_046.html.

[233] Policarpo Junior, "Tem famosos no meio: Polícia apura um bilionário esquema de remessa ilegal de dinheiro ao exterior e já tem nomes de gente graúda" [They Have Famous People Among Them: Police Expedite a Billion-Real Scheme for Remitting Illegal Money Abroad and Already Have the Names of Big-Shots], *Veja on-line*, no. 1,755 (June 12, 2002), http://veja.abril.com.br/120602/p_046.html.

❖ After closing the 137 accounts in New York, the money was remitted to the accounts of 35,000 final beneficiaries, most of them held by juridical people, also located in off-shore havens.

In early 2003, approximately 200 police inquiries into CC-5 accounts were frozen awaiting a decision as to who is competent to continue the investigations.[234] Of a total of about 700 police inquiries concerning money laundering, illegal remittances, and tax evasion, 500 cases remained within the jurisdiction of Foz do Iguaçu. Although the investigations focus on who are involved in the scheme, the ultimate objective is to trace some US$15 billion that left Brazil through CC-5 accounts in Foz do Iguaçu. Brazil's Office of the Attorney General estimates that more than 3,000 people are involved in the so-called Foz do Iguaçu CC-5 accounts scheme.

Other Organized Crime Activities in the TBA

Automobile Smuggling

Smuggling stolen cars is a booming business. Cars are stolen in Brazil and Argentina and taken to Paraguay, and then to Bolivia and beyond. In mid-2001, an Argentine security official stated that an average of 6,000 automobiles are illegally taken out of Argentina every year, and for the most part are sent to Bolivia and Paraguay, specifically Ciudad del Este.[235] The cars arrive in Ciudad del Este no more than 15 hours after being stolen in Buenos Aires. The business in stolen cars, most of which are luxury models, is facilitated not only by lax border controls but also by Paraguayan legislation. Private contracts are accepted as valid instruments under Paraguayan law and can be legalized through a letter-writing procedure, without any requirement for prior documentation. As a result, one can purchase a stolen Mercedes Benz worth US$50,000 for only US$10,000 in Ciudad del Este, or a BMW valued at US$40,000 for only US$7,000.[236] According to Paraguayan authorities, more than half of the 450,000 vehicles registered annually

---

[234] "Investigation on CC-5 Accounts Paralyzed," *Cascavel Hoje* [Foz do Iguaçu], February 5, 2003, as translated for FBIS, "Highlights From the Tri-Border Press for the Week 3-7 February," February 11, 2003 (FBIS Document ID: LAP20030211000124).
[235] Bartolomé, 6.
[236] Bartolomé, 6

in Paraguay were acquired illegally. In addition, automobile theft in Brazil is under the jurisdiction of the State Police, which apparently is not very effective in countering it.[237]

The TBA's two principal centers of reception of stolen vehicles and smuggled goods are Iguaçu Falls on the Brazilian side and Ciudad del Este. They are also a corridor for trafficking in drugs and arms. Some of the illicit cargo passes along an illegally opened road crossing the

Figure 2. Tri-Border Area and Key Roads Leading to It from Major Cities

Iguazú National Park, known as Rodavía del Colono.[238] The Asunción-Paranaguá Highway, which passes near the falls, is also presumably used by smugglers (see Figure 2, Tri-Border Area and Key Roads Leading to It from Major Cities).

---

[237] Silva, 163.
[238] Clarinha Glock, "Brazil-Paraguay: A Full Plate for Journalists," Inter American Press Association, July 19, 2001, http://www.impunidad.com/atrisk/brasil_paraguay7_19_01E.html.

Counterfeiting and Piracy of Products

Argentina and Brazil

Argentina and Brazil are on the Priority Watch List of the copyright-oriented International Intellectual Property Alliance (IIPA) as a result of intellectual property (IP) infringements.[239] Both countries have had repeated problems with copyright protection and enforcement. Street vendors selling fake products and pirated copies of goods ranging from designer-label sneakers to auto parts have long been a part of life in Brazil in particular. More than half of the business software and music CD market in Brazil is pirated, and as much as 40 percent of the cigarettes consumed in Brazil come from the black market. Industry experts also estimate that one-fifth of the drugs on pharmacy shelves is produced illegally.[240] Many of the products being sold in Brazil are known to come into the country from the porous TBA.[241]

Brazilian officials have reported that the power behind the black market is organized crime and international terrorism. The Arab community in the TBA has been tied to the black market trade in pirated goods, particularly CDs. In a series of probes, Paraguayan prosecutors have alleged that pirated CDs were a main funding source for Islamic extremist groups, such as Hizballah and Hamas (see Hizballah Fund-Raising in the TBA, Software Piracy, below).[242]

Paraguay

Paraguay, with a thriving industry of pirated products, limited government support for enforcement, an obstructionist judiciary, and ineffective customs, is considered a nightmare for copyright and trademark owners. The International Anti-Counterfeiting Coalition (IACC) identified Paraguay as a priority foreign country in 1998. Since then, imports of counterfeit CDs and CD-ROMs from Hong Kong, Macau, Thailand, and Malaysia have only increased, making Ciudad del Este the pre-eminent route into Latin America for counterfeits. In February 2000, the IIPA identified Paraguay as the Latin American country causing the most serious problems

---

[239] James Nurton, "Goodbye to A Difficult Year: The World's Leading IP Practices," *Managing Intellectual Property* [London], June 2002, 56–70; *IIPA 2002 "Special 301" Recommendations*, http://www.tetratel.com/custom/downloads/2002_Feb14_PIRACY%20LOSSES.pdf.

[240] Patrice M. Jones, *Chicago Tribune*, "Pirated Goods Cripple Brazil's Economy, But Solutions Seen as Weak," Knight Ridder Tribune News Service, November 4, 2002, 1.

[241] Patrice M. Jones.

[242] Patrice M. Jones.

relating to intellectual property (IP) infringements.[243] It became the only country to rank with China as an IP violator.[244] Paraguay earned this status because it serves as a major trans-shipment point for pirated visual media products from Asia and also produces pirated products, with organized crime elements controlling aspects of production and distribution. In 2000-02, the pirates' strategy changed, with increasing imports of blank recordable CDs and local burners. The IIPA estimates that 104 million recordable CDs were imported in 2001 alone. Many of these discs turn up as pirated music in Brazil.

Total losses from product piracy in Paraguay in 2002 amounted to an estimated US$223.2 million.[245] This figure reflects a nearly twofold increase since 1996, when U.S. companies lost US$117.1 million in 1996 in piracy of products in Paraguay. Much of this criminal activity has been linked to organized criminals based in Korea, Lebanon, Libya, and Taiwan, and the local press has uncovered numerous examples of corruption.

A significant part of the contraband in Ciudad del Este originates in Asia, especially Hong Kong, Taiwan, and Malaysia. These pirated products carry first-line brand names of U.S. or Japanese companies. Three levels of falsification are used depending on the hierarchy of the brand name concerned. For example, the same videocassette recorder can be purchased in Ciudad del Este under the names Panasonic, Sony, or Aiwa.[246] Most of the contraband merchandise leaves Ciudad del Este along the same air, ground, or water routes that were used to enter the city, that is, through Argentine and Brazilian territory. In the case of Brazil, one of the main smuggling routes is along the illegally opened Rodavía del Colono, which cuts through Iguazú National Park. Brazilian authorities have noted the existence of about 100 clandestine airstrips in Paraguay adjacent to the border that are used for contraband and other smuggling to Argentina and Brazil. An estimated US$1.5 billion worth of goods are moved annually.[247]

Contraband transported by boat toward Argentina and Brazil from Ciudad del Este crosses the Rio Paraná and Itaipú Reservoir, which is the 1,350 square-kilometer artificial lake

---

[243] James Nurton, "Goodbye to A Difficult Year: The World's Leading IP Practices."
[244] *IIPA 2002 "Special 301" Recommendations*, http://www.tetratel.com/custom/downloads/ 2002_Feb14_PIRACY%20LOSSES.pdf.
[245] STR 2002 "Special 301" Decisions and IIPA Estimated US Trade Losses Due to Copyright Piracy, http://www.iipa.com/pdf/2002_Jul11_Americas_LOSSES.pdf.
[246] Bartolomé, 6, citing Jorge Camarasa, "Declina la capital del contrabando," *La Nación* [Buenos Aires], April 2, 2000.
[247] Bartolomé, 6, citing *Global Crime: International and Regional Cooperation Among Governments and Gangs Alike*, Transnational Communities Programme, 1998.

on the Brazil-Paraguay border created by the Itaipú Dam. The contraband across the Paraná consists of general merchandise, whereas the contraband transported across the lake consists of stolen automobiles, drugs, and weapons.[248]

Many Brazilian tourists visit Ciudad del Este to purchase cheap consumer goods. Although an estimated 90 percent of the products sold in Ciudad del Este, such as CDs and videos, are counterfeit, their cheap prices make them popular. Contraband and counterfeiting of products in the TBA is centered on about a dozen categories, including electronic equipment, music CDs, videos, computers, athletic shoes, soft drinks, games, jewelry, textiles, perfume, and cigarettes.[249] By 1999, São Paulo tobacco companies had lost an estimated US$600 million as a result of counterfeiting and contraband in Ciudad del Este of Brazilian cigarettes.[250]

The pirating and commercialization of contraband merchandise in Ciudad del Este is facilitated by Paraguayan legislation, which permits the patenting in the National Brand Register of international brand names that are not based in the country.[251] For example, a former minister of industry and commerce patented "aspirin" under his own name and sued the multinational Bayer company when it used the word.[252]

Internet Crime

According to a survey done by the British consulting firm mi2g, a company that serves large banks and insurance companies by monitoring the actions of hackers on the worldwide network of computers, in November 2002 Brazil became the world's largest "exporter" of Internet crimes, including identity theft, credit card fraud, violations of intellectual property (piracy), and the invasion of sites for political protests.[253] Foz do Iguaçu is regarded by Brazilian authorities as one of the main centers of Brazilian Internet crime.[254]

---

[248] Bartolomé, 6.

[249] Bartolomé, 5.

[250] Bartolomé, 5, citing "Brasil, inquieto por el contrabando" [Brazil: Concerned About Contraband], *La Nación* [Buenos Aires], March 4, 2000.

[251] Bartolomé, 6, citing Jorge Camarasa, "Declina la capital del contrabando," *La Nación* [Buenos Aires], April 2, 2000.

[252] Bartolomé, 6, citing Jorge Camarasa.

[253] Marcelos Starobinas, Text *Folha de São Paulo* [São Paulo; Internet version-www; a center-left daily, critical of government in general; top-circulation newspaper], November 20, 2002, as translated for FBIS, "Study Reveals That Brazil is World Leader in Internet Crimes," November 20, 2002 (FBIS Document ID: LAP20021120000057).

[254] International Intellectual Property Alliance, *2003 Special 301 Report: Brazil*, 2003, 62, http://www.iipa.com/rbc/2003/2003SPEC301BRAZIL.pdf.

COMBATING ORGANIZED CRIME AND TERRORIST GROUPS IN THE TBA

The general security forces of Argentina, Brazil, and Paraguay have all been involved in efforts to counter the use of the TBA by organized crime and terrorist groups. On May 31, 1996, the three TBA nations established a "Tripartite Command of the Tri-Border" in an effort to better control commerce and the large transient international population. The command draws on members of the Paraguayan National Police, Argentina's National Gendarmerie or border patrol, Coast Guard (Prefectura Naval), and Federal Police units, as well as representatives from the SIDE, the Argentine Consul's Office in Foz do Iguaçu, the National Aeronautical Police, and the Misiones Provincial Police; and the PF (Brazilian Federal Police), Mountain Infantry Battalion no. 34, the State Intelligence Department, and the Brazilian Consul's Office in Ciudad del Este. In 1998 the Tripartite Command was augmented with a security agreement among the three countries to intensify their fight against terrorism, smuggling, money laundering and drug trafficking.[255]

Despite this joint force, efforts by the TBA governments to counter organized crime and terrorist groups in the TBA have been hindered by institutional problems of corruption, inadequate funding and investigative capabilities, poor training, lack of motivation, inadequate penal codes, and so forth. These factors, which are summarized below, help to explain how organized crime and terrorist groups have operated so profitably in the TBA.

Security Forces

Argentina

Argentina's principal law enforcement agency is the Argentine Federal Police, which is under the jurisdiction of the Ministry of Interior and is involved in countering drugs.[256] The mission of the Argentine National Gendarmerie includes combating drug trafficking, organized

---

[255] Mendel, citing Gendarmería Nacional, *Escuadrón 13 'Iguazú': Estadísticas del funcionamiento del Escuadrón 13 'Iguazú.'* (Puerto de Iguazú, Argentina: Gendarmería Nacional, September, 2001); and "Argentina, Paraguay and Brazil Sign Border Agreement," Press Summary, March 27, 1998, International Policy Institute for Counter-Terrorism, Interdisciplinary Center Herzlia, http://www.ict.org.il; and RLG's Eureka World Law Index, http://eureka.rlg.org/cgi-bin/zgate2.prod.
[256] Scott D. Tollefson, "National Security," Chapter 5 in Rex A. Hudson, ed., *Argentina: A Country Study* (Washington, DC: Library of Congress, Federal Research Division, 1999), unpublished.

crime, and terrorism.[257] The SIDE (Secretariat for State Intelligence) also appears to play a key role in countering terrorist activities. Traditionally, the fight against organized crime is carried out by a special operations unit within the security police and the Judicial Police.[258] The latter operates under the authority of the court prosecutor in each province.[259]

As a highly bureaucratic organization within the executive branch of government, with the exception of the Judicial Police, Argentina's police system, including the special unit, is generally inefficient, and its investigative function is relegated to second place, after maintenance of public order.[260] Lacking, in addition, any special incentives, the police are ineffective in combating organized crime. Even the relatively autonomous but inadequately trained Judicial Police have been unsuccessful in the fight against organized crime.

Occasional combined forces operations in the TBA appear to have caused only a temporary inconvenience for organized crime. For example, in February 2000, Argentina's Secretariat of Internal Security sent 1,000 police officers and four boats of the Naval Prefecture to the TBA to combat contraband.[261] The next month, the Argentine Air Force conducted a surveillance operation that confirmed, within only three days, at least 15 illegal airstrips in the northern Argentine provinces of Misiones and Corrientes. In addition, about 30 unidentified flights mostly coming from Paraguay were detected.[262] Apparently, none were intercepted.

A 28-member Financial Intelligence Unit (Unidad de Información Financiera—UIF), under the Ministry of Justice and Human Rights, began operating in June 2002 as an additional interagency unit to prevent, control, and fight illegal asset laundering activities related to drug and arms trafficking.[263] The establishment of the UIF and the strengthening of anti-money-laundering mechanisms better positioned Argentina to prevent and combat money laundering more effectively, in the assessment of the U.S. Department of State.[264] Despite these measures,

---

[257] The Argentine National Gendarmerie Web site, http://www.gendarmeria.gov.ar/ingles/texto/ing2.htm.
[258] Antolin Almiron, 320.
[259] Kozameh, Ernesto Nicolás, Julio O. Trajtenberg, C.P. Nicolás Kozameh Jr., and Ezequiel Trajtenberg. *Guide to the Argentine Executive, Legislative and Judicial System*, July 15, 2001, http://www.llrx.com/features/argentina.htm.
[260] This paragraph is based in part on Antolin Almiron, 322–27.
[261] Bartolomé, 7.
[262] Bartolomé, 7.
[263] "Ley 25246 Creación de la Unidad de Información Financiera" [Law 25246, Creation of the Financial Information Unit], *Boletín Oficial* [Buenos Aires], May 10, 2000, http://www.imolin.org/argtlaw2.htm.
[264] U.S. Department of State, *International Narcotics Control Strategy Report –2002* (INCSR-2002). Washington, DC: Bureau for International Narcotics and Law Enforcement Affairs, March 2003 (U.S. Department of State, ISCSR-2002), http://www.state.gov/g/inl/rls/nrcrpt/2002/html/17952pf.htm.

however, the Central Bank reportedly has been totally ineffective in prosecuting money laundering.[265]

Corruption is a serious problem at all levels of the Argentine Police.[266] Police are poorly paid, with a starting salary of around US$400 (400 pesos) a month rising to about US$2,000 (2,000 pesos) a month for a captain. For the past 20 years, the Argentine police reportedly have been involved in organized crime. For example, the white van used in the AMIA attack was traced to Police Commissioner Juan José Ribelli, who had long been suspected of using his position to traffic in stolen automobiles to Paraguay.[267] In 2002, a lawyer at the Center for the Prevention of Police Repression (Coordinadora Contra la Represión Policial e Institucional—Correpi), stated that "in the last decade, there has not been any major illegal business without police participation, from prostitution to gambling, robbery, or kidnapping."[268]

The inadequacy of Argentina's penal code for combating organized crime seems typical of the three TBA countries. Argentina's Penal Code has not defined organized crime legally; its penal law is, in fact, "typical," meaning that criminal behavior must be exactly defined in the Penal Code.[269] Judicial and legal analogy in penal matters is forbidden. The Penal Code lacks the necessary doctrine of "illicit association," which defines organized crime, such as a conspiracy by three or more persons to commit offenses through an organization. With the exception of laws related to drug matters, Argentina does not have special laws to fight against organized crime.[270]

---

[265] Pedro Oviedo, "En la Triple Frontera se lavan doce mil millones de dólares al año del narcotráfico, según un informe official" [In the Triple Border US$12 billion Is Laundered Per Year From Narcotics Trafficking, According to An Official Report],www.MisionesOnLine.net, no. 745 (July 8, 2001), http://misionesonline.net/paginas/action.lasso?-database=noticias3&-layout=web&-response=noticia.html&id=11349&autorizado=si&-search; and "The Fight Against Money Laundering," *La Nación* [Buenos Aires; Internet version-www], February 24, 2003, as translated for FBIS, "Argentina: Daily Calls for Full Support of Agency Created to Fight Money Laundering," February 24, 2003 (FBIS Document ID: LAP20030224000052),.

[266] This discussion is based in part on U.S. Department of State, "Argentina," *Country Reports on Human Rights Practices – 2001* (Washington, DC: Bureau of Democracy, Human Rights, and Labor, U.S. Department of State, March 4, 2002), http://www.state.gov/g/drl/rls/hrrpt/2001/wha/8278.htm.

[267] Junger, 199.

[268] "Delinquent; Politics in Argentina (Argentina's Crime Wave)," *The Economist* [London], October 5, 2002.

[269] This paragraph is based in part on Hugo Antolin Almiron, "Organized Crime: A Perspective from Argentina." Chapter 14 in Jay S. Albanese, Dilip K. Das, and Arvind Verma, eds., *Organized Crime: World Perspectives* (Upper Saddle River, New Jersey: Prentice Hall, 2003), 318–19.

[270] Antolin Almiron, 327.

Brazil

Public security in Brazil is largely the responsibility of state governments. In contrast with its Argentine counterpart, Brazil's PF (Federal Police) force is very small and primarily investigative.[271] It plays only a minor role in routine law enforcement. Its purpose is to investigate criminal offenses of an interstate or international nature; to prevent and suppress illicit traffic in narcotics and related drugs; to perform the functions of a coast guard (enforcement only), air police, and border patrol; and to perform the functions of the judicial police.[272] A task force made up of the Civil and Military Police, the PF, the Federal Highway Police, the Municipal Guard, and, in some cases, the Armed Forces has operated in Foz do Iguaçu since April 2001.[273] The frequency of money laundering around the region of Foz de Iguaçu is of concern to the Brazilian government because of the TBA's high occurrences of intellectual property violations and illicit commerce, and because the TBA is believed to be a haven for smuggling and arms trafficking.[274]

Although some Brazilian police forces are known to be highly professional, a December 2000 Argentine report indicates that a supposed connection has been established between the Civil Police of Foz do Iguaçu and a narcotics network that operates in the Brazilian and Paraguayan parts of the TBA. The chief of Civil Police of Foz do Iguaçu, who has been suspended, was involved.[275] The effectiveness of Brazil's police forces in fighting organized crime and terrorist groups in the TBA is hindered by a general lack of respect for human rights (which makes much of the population fear the police at least as much as most Brazilians fear the criminals), widespread corruption and involvement in crime, and a general failure of the Brazilian government to address its serious problems.

---

[271] This discussion is based in part on Scott D. Tollefson, "National Security," Chapter 5 in Rex A. Hudson, ed., Brazil: A Country Study (Washington, DC: Library of Congress, Federal Research Division, 1998), 400–402; and U.S. Department of State, "Brazil," Country Reports on Human Rights Practices – 2001 (Washington, DC: Bureau of Democracy, Human Rights, and Labor, U.S. Department of State, March 4, 2002), http://www.state.gov/g/drl/rls/hrrpt/2001/wha/8305.htm.

[272] Silva, 169.

[273] Miriam Karam, São Paulo Valor [financial daily, published jointly by the Folha and Globo media conglomerates; Internet version-www], May 20, 2002, as translated for FBIS, "Brazil: Federal Police Denies Presence of Terrorist Cells in Foz do Iguaçu" (FBIS Document ID: LAP20020520000040).

[274] U.S. Department of State, International Narcotics Control Strategy Report –2002 (Washington, DC: Bureau for International Narcotics and Law Enforcement Affairs, March 2003), http://www.state.gov/g/inl/rls/nrcrpt/2002/html/17952pf.htm.

[275] Oviedo, citing Dr. Guido Rauber Lavado de Dinero: Triple Frontera —Work Paper N° 1, Prevención de Adicciones y Control de Drogas [Subsecretary of Drug Control and Prevention of Addictions], Ministry of Public Health of Misiones Province, Argentina, updated version of December 31, 2000 (original date, August 2, 1999).

The Brazilian government's attitude toward the existence of a terrorist problem in the TBA is also a factor. The government has insisted that there is no evidence of terrorist financing in the area, and it has been generally dismissive of reports of terrorists operating in the area.[276] Nevertheless, Article 4 of Decree 3,755, issued on February 19, 2001, blocks all funds from being sent from Brazil to Osama bin Laden or to companies, associations, or people linked to him. At least three of the decree's articles refer to the Arab terrorist threat.[277]

In March 1998, Brazil's Congress adopted a law authorizing the shooting down of intercepted airplanes that fail to obey signals of the intercepting pilots who patrol the border with Paraguay, but the measure has yet to be implemented. In May 2001, in an effort to interdict contraband, the PF established an air base in Foz do Iguaçu, from where its aircraft patrol the Rio Paraná and the Itaipú Reservoir.[278] On August 22, 2002, in an effort to strengthen border controls, the PF began suppressing illegal activities in the TBA's Friendship Bridge area, specifically along the Paraná.[279] The operation was aimed at preventing smugglers and traffickers from using the river for their operations after customs officers increased the traffic control on the head of the bridge. Joaquim Mesquita, chief of the Foz do Iguaçu PF, reported that the main PF drug enforcement actions in 2002 in the TBA included the confiscation of 12.7 tons of marijuana and of 30 kilograms of cocaine mostly coming from Bolivia and

---

[276] For example, see "Brazil: Minister Denies Existence of Terrorist Cell in Triborder Area," BBC Monitoring Americas—Political [London], November 9, 2002, citing text of report by Edson Luiz published by Brazil's Agencia Estado, November 9, 2002; Carmen Gentile, UPI, "Brazil Denies Terror Groups in Region," *The Washington Times*, November 11, 2002, http://www.washingtontimes.com; Hala Kilani and Cilina Nasser, "Brazil Dismisses US-Israeli Terror Claims; Ambassador Says 'Tri-border Area' Is Well Policed," *The Daily Star* [Independent Beirut paper; Internet version-www], February 14, 2003, as transcribed for FBIS, "Brazilian Ambassador to Lebanon Denies Terrorist Activities in Tri-Border Area," February 14, 2003 (FBIS Document ID: GMP20030214000022).
[277] Edson Luiz, "Brasil bloqueou bens de Bin Laden antes dos EUA" [Brazil Blocks bin Laden Funds Before the USA], Oestadao.com, Setembro 24, 2001, http://www.estadao.com.br /agestado/noticias/2001/set/24/305.htm.
[278] Bartolomé, 7.
[279] "Brazilian Federal Police (PF) Launches Gigantic Operation—Ciudad del Este," *Vanguardia* [Ciudad del Este], August 26, 2002, as translated for FBIS, "Highlights: Brazil - Paraguay Triborder Press 26-30 Aug 02," Tri-Border Press Highlights, September 2, 2002 (FBIS Document ID: LAP20020902000038).

Colombia.[280] Undoubtedly, those seizures constitute only a small fraction of the drug traffic. In late 2002, Brazilian authorities reinforced security controls in the Friendship Bridge area by installing two 360-degree panoramic vision surveillance posts (POVs) and by posting 70 agents to the area.[281]

Paraguay

Information on capabilities of the 200-member Paraguayan police force in Ciudad del Este is lacking, but it is clearly not an effective force, and it is suspected of corruption.[282] A general lack of confidence in the local police may be reflected by the fact that the city's 6,000 shops, 36 banks, and 15 money exchanges all have their private guards. By October 2001, as authorities in Paraguay increased surveillance of the country's Arab immigrants, there were charges that police were extorting large sums of money from some merchants in the TBA in return for not detaining them.[283]

At the national level, the Secretariat for Prevention and Investigation of Terrorism in Paraguay (Secretaría de Prevención e Investigación del Terrorismo de Paraguay—Seprinte) has been in the forefront of operations and arrests carried out in the Paraguayan sector of the TBA since the September 11, 2001 attacks in the United States. This relatively small antiterrorist organization is a department of the police and works with anti-money-laundering agencies, including the Financial Analysis Unit (Unidad de Análisis Financiera—UAF).[284] The establishment of the UAF under the Attorney General's office in July 2002 was expected by the U.S. Department of State to enhance cooperation at the working level and to improve the Attorney General's ability to investigate money laundering and terrorist financing.[285] The UAF,

---

[280] "Federal Police's Annual Report," *A Gazeta do Iguacu* [Foz do Iguaçu], January 24, 2003, as translated for FBIS, "Tri-Border Press for the Week of 23-31 January," Tri-Border Press Highlights, February 4, 2003 (FBIS Document ID: LAP20030204000134).

[281] "Surveillance System on Friendship Bridge," A Gazeta do Iguaçu, November 6, 2002, as translated for FBIS, "Highlights: Brazil - Paraguay Triborder Press 4-15 Nov 02," November 21, 2002 (FBIS Document ID: LAP20021121000006).

[282] This paragraph is based in information from Ricardo Grinbaum, "In Paraguay, Smugglers' Paradise," *World Press Review* 43, no.1 (January 1996): 25–26 (reprinted from *Veja*).

[283] Bill Rogers, "Arabs Accuse Paraguay Police Of Extortion," *Middle East News Online* [Durham, North Carolina], October 4, 2001.

[284] Location: Juan E. O'Leary 165, esq Benjamín Constant, Asunción (Tel.: (+595) 21 452 411/412; Fax: (+595) 21 451 635; E-Mail: seprelad@conexion.com.py).

[285] This paragraph is based in part on U.S. Department of State, ISCSR-2002.

which is recognized by the U.S. government and the Egmont Group as a financial intelligence unit, has purview only over financial institutions.[286]

In addition to establishing the UAF, the Paraguayan government has carried out limited efforts to combat terrorist financing. Nevertheless, Paraguay has limited resources to investigate and prosecute money-laundering cases. Investigations are carried out by a small financial crimes investigative unit, the Unit for Investigating Financial Data (Unidad de Investigación de Datos Financieros—UIDF). Because there are only about 200 prosecutors nationwide for a population of 5.5 million, money-laundering investigations in Paraguay are assigned to a single prosecutor. Furthermore, government corruption is an ongoing problem related to Paraguay's money laundering and money-laundering investigations.[287]

Other than the draft Antiterrorist Law that was introduced in the Chamber of Deputies in 2002 and remains under consideration, the Paraguayan government currently has no specific laws criminalizing terrorism or terrorist financing.[288] Paraguay has adopted provisions to cover conduct that would be considered terrorist acts, but most of these acts do not carry a sentence of more than five years, nor are they considered predicate offenses for money laundering. Although some existing legislation allows for counterterrorist police operations, the lack of any legislation specifically targeting terrorist activities has greatly impeded the efforts of the Paraguayan Antiterrorist Police. Paraguay also lacks the investigative capabilities to track the terrorists' financial transactions.

The TBA's Immigration Control Problem

The TBA is known for its lax immigration controls. It is common knowledge that anyone in the region can easily obtain a false passport, birth certificate, driver's license, and other documents through corrupt officials. Relatively few members of the Asian, Arab, and other ethnic communities in the TBA are believed to be legally registered. Paraguay's Vice Interior Minister Mario Agustin Sapriza pointed out on May 3, 2001, that the Immigrations Department

---

[286] This paragraph is based in part on U.S. Department of State, ISCSR-2002.
[287] This paragraph is based in part on U.S. Department of State, ISCSR-2002.
[288] "Paraguay: US Official Says Tri-border Area Source of Islamic Terrorism Funding," BBC Monitoring Americas – Political [London], May 25, 2002, citing *ABC Color* Web site, May 23, 2002.

is where most difficulties are found in preventing the TBA from being used by Islamic extremists.[289]

Arrests in Ciudad del Este in 2001 showed how typical it is for suspected Islamic extremists in the TBA to be without valid identity documents. One individual arrested in May by Paraguay's Federal Police at the Ciudad del Este Airport had 17 fake Lebanese passports in his possession.[290] On September 21, Paraguayan police carried out two operations in Ciudad del Este and nearby Encarnación in which 17 Arabs were arrested, all of whom had false identity documents and had no entry documents registered by the Department of Immigration.[291] The FBI identified three of arrested individuals as having close ties to Hamas and the Lebanese Al-Kaffir group. Reportedly, they collected funds for these terrorist groups to support terrorist plots against the United States.[292] Another who escaped the police round-up in Encarnación is the Egyptian Khaled Ta Qe El Din, who is an important figure in the Arab community of Foz do Iguaçu and Ciudad del Este and believed to be a bin Laden follower and a member of an Egyptian terrorist organization.[293]

In early October 2001, high-level sources in Argentina's Ministry of Interior called Brazil's immigration control system for the TBA a problem.[294] Argentina places its emphasis on immigration control at the border crossings, while Brazil's control operations are located somewhat deeper inside its territory. In 2002, Brazilian authorities established controls on the roads several kilometers from Foz do Iguaçu.

---

[289] *ABC Color* [Internet version-www], May 4, 2001, as translated for FBIS, "Paraguay: Vice Interior Minister Confirms Presence of 'Dormant Islamic Terrorist Cells'" (FBIS Document ID: LAP20010505000002).

[290] Mario Daniel Montoya, "War on Terrorism Reaches Paraguay's Triple Border," *Jane's Intelligence Review* 13, no. 12 (December 2001): 13; and "Policiais viajam em vôos internos argentinos" [Police fly on internal Argentine flights], Oestado.com.br, September 19, 2001, http://www.estadao.com.br/agestado/noticias/2001/set/19/207.htm.

[291] James Mack, Deputy Assistant for International Narcotics and Law Enforcement Affairs, "Providing Support to Counternarcotics and Other Anti-Crime Efforts," Testimony Before the House Committee on International Relations Subcommittee on the Western Hemisphere, Washington, DC, October 10, 2001, http://www.state.gov/g/inl/rls/rm/ 2001/sep_oct/6215.htm; and Bartolomé, 14, citing "Juez confirmó la prisión de los 13 árabes" [Judge Confirms Prison for the 13 Arabs], *Noticias*, September 25, 2001. According to the list released to the press, the 11 who were charged included: Mohamed Jassin, Yehya Hamed Kaddoura, Abdel Nasser Waked, Assen Mohammed Waked, Yazzed Khalil Abu El Hawa, Rateb Ahmad Ayoub, Samir Nazih Jbara, Jehya Fallez Hussein, Hassan Abdalah Halawi, Kassen Mohamed Fawaz, and Sufián Asfour Mahamad Asfour.

[292] Bartolomé, 15, citing "Paraguay lanza operativo contra el terrorismo" [Paraguay launches operation against terrorism], *El Nuevo Herald* [Miami], September 23, 2001.

[293] Bartolomé, 15, citing "Egipcio está sendo investigado pela PF" [Egyptian is being investigated by PF], *O Estado de São Paulo*, September 24, 2001.

[294] *La Nación* [Buenos Aires], October 3, 2001, as translated for FBIS, "National Border Guard Commander: Tri-Border Area Hotbed of Sleeper Cells," October 3, 2001 (FBIS Document ID: LAP20011003000015).

CONCLUDING POINTS

The TBA as a Haven and Base for Islamic Terrorist Groups

This assessment of open sources pertaining to the TBA during the 1999-June 2003 period concludes that:

❖ various Islamic terrorist groups, including the Egyptian Al-Jihad (Islamic Jihad) and Al-Gama'a al-Islamiyya (Islamic Group), Hamas, Hizballah, and al Qaeda, probably have a presence in the TBA;

❖ Hizballah and al Qaeda are probably cooperating in the region, but definitive proof of this collaboration, in the form of a specific document, did not surface in this review;

❖ Islamic terrorist groups are using the TBA for purposes of safe haven, fund-raising, money laundering, recruitment, training, plotting, and other terrorist-related activities;

❖ terrorism within the TBA by Islamic terrorist groups has been limited to selective, mafia-like assassinations of business or community leaders who may be opposing their interests;

❖ the Islamic fundamentalist groups' activities in the TBA are in support of their international organizations and the Islamic jihad against the United States and U.S. allies;

❖ Hizballah has reaped hundreds of millions of dollars in profits from narcotics and arms trafficking, product piracy, and other illicit activities in the TBA;

❖ a substantial number of members of the Islamic terrorist groups in the TBA have probably moved out of the region since late 2001 to other areas of South America, such as Chile, Uruguay, and Venezuela, where they may be under less pressure by security forces than in the TBA; and

❖ if TBA-based Hizballah and al Qaeda operatives are plotting any anti-U.S. terrorist attacks, their most likely targets would be U.S. embassies and consulates in South America.

The TBA as a Center for Organized Crime

This assessment also concludes that:

❖ the TBA is highly popular with other organized crime groups, which use the region to launder billions of dollars every year and to earn multi-million-dollar profits by engaging in narcotics and arms trafficking and other illicit activities;

❖ an informal tripartite alliance exists among the Islamic terrorist groups, the organized crime mafias, and the many corrupt government or police officials in the TBA and elsewhere in the TBA countries;

❖ this informal alliance appears to be primarily oriented toward reaping multi-million-dollar profits from illicit activities;

❖ various Chinese Mafia groups operate in the TBA and are attempting to expand their activities into Argentina and elsewhere;

❖ the Chinese and Russian (Chechen) mafias reportedly are collaborating with the Islamic terrorist groups in the region, especially with al Qaeda;

❖ the Hong Kong Mafia, which has close relations with the Hizballah network in the TBA, is particularly active in the product-piracy business; and

❖ indigenous Argentine, Brazilian, and Paraguayan mafia groups are also actively involved in the TBA.

Efforts to Counter Organized Crime and Terrorism in the TBA

This assessment also concludes that:

❖ widespread corruption at all levels of government and police in the three TBA countries is facilitating the activities of the Islamic terrorist groups and organized crime in the TBA;

❖ the capabilities of the security and investigative forces in the TBA are inadequate for ridding the region of the Islamic terrorist groups, organized crime mafias, and corrupt officials who do business with them; and

❖ laws for combating terrorist fund-raising, money laundering, organized crime activities in general, and official corruption are also inadequate.

APPENDIX

Alleged Operatives of Islamic Fundamentalist Groups in the TBA

Barakat, Assad Ahmad Mohamad (Hizballah)

Assad Mohamed Barakat, 37, is generally identified as Hizballah's military (i.e., terrorist) operations chief in the TBA, as well as its chief fund-raising officer in the Southern Cone. The U.S. Department of State has also reportedly identified him as connected to the al-Gama'a al-Islamiyya (Egyptian Islamic Group).[295] He is also believed to be heavily involved in Hizballah funding operations in the region. Following the September 11, 2001, terrorist attacks in the United States, an international arrest warrant was issued for his arrest, and as a result Barakat fled the TBA in October 2001. He was indicted in Paraguay on charges of association for criminal purposes, abetment of crime, and tax evasion.[296] Brazilian authorities arrested Barakat in Foz do Iguaçu on June 22, 2002, and imprisoned him in Brasília, where he has been awaiting a decision from the Federal Supreme Court on an extradition request from Paraguay.[297] In mid-December 2002, the plenum of the Brazilian Federal Supreme Court ruled to extradite Barakat to Paraguay.[298]

---

[295] "Barakat To Be Extradited: Slippery Barakat Caught by Federal Police Hands," *Última Hora*, June 24, 2002, as translated by FBIS, "Highlights: Paraguay Press," June 24, 2002, (FBIS Document ID: LAP20020624000088).

[296] "Another Serious Charge Pending Against Barakat," *Vanguardia* [Ciudad del Este; Internet version-www], June 26, 2002, as translated for FBIS, "Paraguay Press Highlights," June 26, 2002 (FBIS Document ID: LAP20020626000113); and Héctor Rojas and Pablo Vergara, *La Tercera de la Hora* [Santiago; a conservative, pro-business, top-circulation daily, Internet version-www], November 8, 2001, as translated for FBIS, "Chilean Police Examine Link to Alleged Triborder Hizballah Financial Network," November 8, 2001 (FBIS Document ID: LAP20011108000085).

[297] Jose Maschio, reporting on telephone interview between Assad Ahmad Barakat and Agencia Folha on November 18, 2002, from his prison cell in Brasília, *Folha de São Paulo* (Internet version-www), November 19, 2002, as translated for FBIS, "Brazil: Barakat Denies Involvement in Terrorism; Views 'Economic Plot' Against Him" (FBIS Document ID: LAP20021119000039).

[298] "Brazilian Federal Supreme Court Rule To Extradite Barakat," *ABC Color* [Internet version-www], December 20, 2002, as translated for FBIS, December 20, 2002 (FBIS Document ID: LAP20021220000015).

A Lebanese by birth, Barakat left civil-war-torn Lebanon at age 17 and emigrated to Paraguay with his father. After a few years as a street peddler, he opened Apollo Import-Export, a stall in the Page shopping gallery in Ciudad del Este. Since then, he reportedly has accumulated numerous companies, including the Mondial (World) Engineering and Construction company, with offices in Ciudad del Este and Beirut, as well as numerous properties. Ahmad is the brother of priest Akraam Ahmad Barakat, who reportedly is also a high-ranking leader of Iran's Hizballah.[299]

Barakat's Paraguayan passport reportedly indicates that he was last in the United States in April 2000. His visa was revoked after his name appeared on the U.S. Department of State's list of "suspected terrorists." Barakat has acknowledged owning businesses in Chile and the United States (Miami and New York).[300]

Fayad, Sobhi Mahmoud (Hizballah)

Sobhi Mahmoud Fayad, who claims to be a Lebanese businessman but is widely reported to be a key Hizballah operative, was arrested at the Page shopping gallery in Ciudad del Este on November 8, 2001, on charges of being an alleged member of an organization that remits funds to the Islamic Middle East armed struggle.[301] Documents found at the Apollo shop owned by Assad Ahmad Barakat allegedly incriminate Sobhi Fayad. On the basis of the documents, it was alleged that Sobhi Fayad, who had not paid taxes since 1992, was sending large sums of money to banks in Lebanon almost daily. He remained under arrest in the Special Operations Police Force unit in Asunción, together with his brother Salhed Fayad, until he was released on bail in early October 2002. On November 21, 2002, Sobhi Mahmoud Fayad submitted to public trial for

---

[299] Special Correspondents Vladimir Jara Vera and Dany Ortiz, *ABC Color* [Internet version], December 23, 1999, as translated for FBIS, "Police Conduct Operation to Intimdate Islamic Extremists," December 23, 1999 (FBIS Document ID: FTS19991223001521).

[300] *La Tercera de la Hora* [Internet version-www], November 14, 2001, as translated for FBIS, "Hizballah-Linked Businessman Acknowledges Having Businesses in Chile, US," November 14, 2001 (FBIS Document ID: LAP20011114000075200).

[301] *ABC Color* [Web site], November 9, 2001, as cited by "Paraguay: Lebanese Man with Alleged Hezbollah Links Arrested in Ciudad del Este," BBC Monitoring, November 9, 2001.

tax evasion. He was indicted for running a business without accounting books, using falsified public documents, and tax evasion in 1998 and 1999.[302]

Paraguayan authorities reportedly believe that Sobhi Fayad, along with Barakat and fugitive Ali Hassan Abdallah, are the coordinators of a Hizballah financial network in the TBA. In addition, Fayad is a brother of an important Hizballah member in Lebanon. Authorities regard Fayad as one of the main Hizballah chiefs assigned to the TBA.[303] Police found in his possession documents for funds sent to Canada and Lebanon. Fayad's influence within the Lebanese community in the TBA was emphasized by reports that he was seen in the company of the new Lebanese ambassador in Paraguay, Hicham Hamdam, who presented his credential in Asunción in October 2001, on various occasions when the diplomat attended local activities. A letter that Fayad received from Lebanon allegedly proves that in 2000 alone he sent more than US$3.5 million to the "Martyr" Social Beneficent Organization, which is linked to the Hizballah and which looks after children whose parents died at the service of the Hizballah and who are considered martyrs.[304] Investigators confirmed the presence of Fayad at an Al-Mukawama operations center. According to Interior Ministry sources, he appears in one of the surveillance photos chatting with Iman Tareb Khasraji (on left in photo) in early November 2001.[305]

Fayad initially became a fugitive in October 1998.[306] Paraguayan authorities had arrested him in 1998, while he was

---

[302] *ABC Color* [Internet version-www], November 22, 2002, as translated for FBIS (FBIS Document ID: LAP20021122000047).

[303] Libanês preso no Paraguai é "peso pesado" do Hezbollah, diz polícia" (Lebanese Imprisoned in Paraguay Is a Hizballah Heavyweight, Police Say), estadao.com.br [Website of *O Estado de São Paulo*], November 9, 2001.

[304] Roberto Cosso, "Extremistas receberam US$50 mi de Foz do Iguaçu" (Extremists Received US$50 million from Foz do Iguaçu), *Folha de S. Paulo*, December 3, 2001; and *ABC Color* [Internet version-www], May 28, 2002, as translated for FBIS, "Paraguay: Daily Reports More Evidence of Barakat's Contributions to Hizballah," May 28, 2002 (FBIS Document ID: LAP20020528000073).

[305] *ABC Color* [Internet Version-www], January 16, 2002, as translated for FBIS, "Paraguay: Court Investigates Hizballah Base Photos" (FBIS, LAP20020116000091).

[306] Bartolomé, 15.

observing the U.S. Embassy in Asunción, either before or after requesting an appointment in the facility. He was later released after cooperating with authorities.[307] In October 1999, Fayad was again arrested in front of the U.S. Embassy in Asunción, after having requested a visa. On that occasion, he was questioned on the basis of the suspicions of U.S. officials, but he was later again released for lack of evidence against him.

Mehri, Ali Khalil (Hizballah)

The relationship between the TBA underworld and Middle East terrorism became clearer in February 2000, when Paraguayan authorities arrested Ali Khalil Mehri, 32, a newly naturalized Paraguayan citizen born in Lebanon. Considered one of the principal Hizballah fund-raisers in the TBA, Mehri was arrested during a police raid of his apartment at the Panorama II building in Ciudad del Este on February 25, 2000. Shortly thereafter, he escaped and has eluded Interpol's attempt to capture him.[308] At the time that Mehri disappeared, Argentine authorities were interested in questioning him in connection with the two unsolved bombings of Israeli targets in Buenos Aires in the early 1990s—that of the Israeli Embassy on March 17, 1992, and a Jewish community center (AMIA) on July 18, 1994.[309]

Reportedly, Merhi had access codes to restricted Web sites that promote international terrorism, and when they raided his apartment, police found software that he allegedly was distributing to raise money for Al-Muqawamah.[310] The software features film footage of terrorist attacks and interviews with suicide bombers before they died. It also provides a bank account number in Lebanon, where money could be sent to support Al-Muqawamah. In a certified

---

[307] "Libanês preso no Paraguai."
[308] *ABC Color*, November 5, 2001, as translated for FBIS, "Barchini's Calls Under Scrutiny, New Antiterrorist Officials," November 5, 2001 (FBIS Document ID: LAP20011105000019).
[309] Kevin G. Hall, "Officials Link Pirated Goods in Paraguay to Terrorism: Money Sent on to Hezbollah," *San Diego Union –Tribune*, April 15, 2001, A19.
[310] Hall, *San Diego Union –Tribune.*

translation of the CD's Arabic contents, an unidentified radical leader exhorts listeners to strike at the United States and Israel.[311]

Other documents seized during the raid included fund-raising forms for a group in the Middle East named Al-Shahid, ostensibly dedicated to "the protection of families of martyrs and prisoners," as well as documents of money transfers to Canada, Chile, Lebanon, and the United States of more than US$700,000.[312] British intelligence subsequently identified Mehri as a potential al Qaeda financier.[313] Paraguayan authorities charged Mehri with piracy of computer programs and CDs and with selling millions of dollars of counterfeit software and funneling the proceeds to Hizballah. Apparently aided by his large campaign contributions to powerful members of Paraguay's ruling Colorado Party, Mehri escaped from prison in June 2000 and fled to Syria.[314] In late September 2001, he was located in Syria, and Paraguay asked Interpol to arrest him, but he managed to escape.[315]

Mukhlis, El Said Hassan Ali Mohamed (al-Gama'a al-Islamiyya)

Argentina's Secretariat for State Intelligence (SIDE) has investigated the Egyptian Al-Sa'id Ali Hasan Mukhlis (also spelled Mokhles), 31, who has been identified as having contacts with Saudi Arabian members of a group of Osama bin Laden militants in the TBA. Mukhlis, an Egyptian who had trained in Afghanistan and lived in Saudi Arabia and was a member of the Islamic fundamentalist group al-Gama'a al-Islamiyya, was suspected of participating in the massacre of 62 foreign tourists at Luxor, Egypt, on November 17, 1997. A native of the coastal city of Port Said, Mukhlis left Egypt in the early 1990s, fearing random arrests of Al-Gama'a members.

---

[311] Hall, *San Diego Union –Tribune.*

[312] "Comandos terroristas se refugian en la triple frontera" (Terrorist "Commandos" Hide in the Triborder Region), *El País* [Colombia], November 9, 2001.

[313] Roslyn A. Mazer, "From T-Shirts to Terrorism: That Fake Nike Swoosh May Be Helping to Fund Bin Laden's Network," *Washington Post*, September 30, 2001, B2. The U.S. Embassy cancelled the visa issued to Deputy Angel Ramón Barchini to enter the United States because of his alleged links with suspicious Arab extremists, including Mehri, whose escape he allegedly abetted. See *ABC Color*, November 5, 2001, as translated for FBIS, "Barchini's Calls Under Scrutiny, New Antiterrorist Officials," November 5, 2001 (FBIS Document ID: LAP20011105000019).

[314] Roslyn A. Mazer, "From T-Shirts to Terrorism: That Fake Nike Swoosh May Be Helping to Fund Bin Laden's Network," *Washington Post*, September 30, 2001, B2.

[315] Bartolomé, 11, citing "Detectan en Siria presencia de megapirata libanés prófugo" [Lebanese megapirate fugitive detected in Syria], *ABC*, September 27, 2001.

Argentine security suspected that the detonators used in the 1994 AMIA attack were secured in the TBA and linked Mukhlis to that operation. Argentine security believed that Mukhlis established terrorist cells in Foz do Iguaçu to raise funds, to manufacture counterfeit documents, and to maintain contact with Hamas and Hizballah sympathizers. After living with his family in Foz do Iguaçu in 1998, Mukhlis was arrested at a border control station in El Chuy, Uruguay, on the Brazilian-Uruguayan border on January 26, 1999, as he tried to leave Brazil using a fake Malaysian passport. Contacted by border-control authorities, the CIA reportedly requested that he be detained on charges of having participated in the 1997 terrorist attack that killed 62 U.S. and European tourists in Luxor. At the time of his arrest, Mukhlis was allegedly en route to Europe for a meeting with another al Qaeda terrorist. Egypt immediately began a lengthy legal struggle to extradite Mukhlis. In mid-1999 Egypt demanded that Uruguay extradite Mukhlis on the accusation in absentia of having participated in the Luxor attack. Uruguay's Supreme Court approved the extradition request in early May 2003.

Mukhlis' wife, Sahar (Sarrah) Mohamed Hassam Abud Hamanra, was arrested along with her husband in 1999 but immediately released. At the time of her arrest in Uruguay, Hamanra produced Brazilian documentation that Brazil's Federal Police (PF), which had already investigated her for one month, declared false. She is on the list of 100 people that the FBI wanted to interview after September 11. Just hours after the hijacked planes crashed into the World Trade Center and the Pentagon, the FBI reportedly requested South American security services to intensify efforts to locate Mukhlis' wife. Law enforcement sources were quoted in the report as saying that Hamanra could be the contact between al Qaeda and the Arab community in the TBA.[316]

According to official sources, citing the SIDE, Mukhlis received military training in Afghanistan from Al-Jama'at al-Islamiyah in the 1980s. He was later sent to Foz do Iguaçu by bin Laden. In that Brazilian city, Mukhlis allegedly "formed terrorist cells to collect funds for the

---

[316] Martin Arostegui, "Search for Bin Laden links looks south," www.autentico.org [UPI via COMTEX], October 12, 2001.

Middle East and to conduct logistical support activities, such as forging passports or other documents. That false documentation was meant for activists in the Islamic Jihad." Furthermore, officials asserted that "he had a mission to make contact with Hamas and Hizballah sympathizers" in Ciudad del Este, Foz do Iguaçu, and São Paulo.

In a ruling made public on October 5, 2001, an Uruguayan appeals court approved the extradition of Mukhlis, conditioning its approval on commitments from Egypt to not apply the death penalty, to respect due process, and to not try him on the charge of falsification of documents, for which he was already convicted in Uruguay. However, an appeal of the ruling to the Supreme Court was expected to take another 12 months. The appeals court reportedly indicated that Mukhlis was trained in Afghan camps commanded by Osama bin Laden.[317]

al-Qadi, Marwan 'Adnan ("Marwan al-Safadi") (Hizballah)

Marwan 'Adnan al-Qadi ("Marwan al-Safadi"), 40, participated in the bombing of the World Trade Center on February 26, 1993. He was arrested in November 1996 in connection with a plot by Islamic groups in the TBA to blow up the U.S. Embassy in Paraguay that month. Police who raided his apartment in Ciudad del Este found it filled with explosives, pistols equipped with silencers, double-barreled rifles, false Canadian and U.S. passports, and a large amount of cash. Al-Qadi fled to Asunción, where Paraguayan police detained him. Two days later, U.S. officials escorted him to the United States.[318]

Although extradited to the United States and sentenced to 18 months in prison, al-Qadi was deported to Canada, where he received a nine-year prison sentence for drug trafficking. Al-Qadi escaped from Canada's prisons three times and finally succeeding in escaping from prison in Montreal, with the help of Hizballah elements in that area, and fleeing to South America with a false passport. Arrested by Brazilian authorities, he again escaped three times from prison in Brazil before reaching Ciudad del Este.[319]

---

[317] *El Nuevo Herald* [Miami], October 6, 2001, from AFP; *New York Times*, November 27, 2001, citing a report published on October 5, 2001, in the Uruguayan daily *El Observador*.
[318] Humberto Trezzi, "EUA pressionam Brasil a colaborar" [USA pressures Brazil to collaborate], *Zero Hora*, September 19, 2001.
[319] Trezzi, *Zero Hora*.

SELECTIVE BIBLIOGRAPHY

"Al-Qaeda and Argentina," *Jane's Intelligence Digest* [London], October 26, 2001.

Albanese, Jay S., Dilip K. Das, and Arvind Verma, eds., *Organized Crime: World Perspectives.* Upper Saddle River, New Jersey: Prentice Hall, 2003.

Almiron, Hugo Antolin. "Organized Crime: A Perspective from Argentina." Chapter 14 in Jay S. Albanese, Dilip K. Das, and Arvind Verma, eds., *Organized Crime: World Perspectives.* Upper Saddle River, New Jersey: Prentice Hall, 2003, 317–29.

Anderson, Martin. "Al-Qaeda Across the Americas," *Insight on the News*, November 26, 2002, 20-22.

Argentina. "Ley 25246 Creación de la Unidad de Información Financiera" [Law 25246, Creation of the Financial Information Unit]. *Boletín Oficial* [Buenos Aires], May 10, 2000. http://www.imolin.org/argtlaw2.htm.

Bagley, Bruce Michael. *Globalization and Transnational Organized Crime: The Russian Mafia in Latin America and the Caribbean*, October 31, 2001. http://www.mamacoca.org/ feb2002/art_bagley_globalization_organized_crime_en.html#fn1.

Bartolomé, Mariano César. *Amenzas a la seguridad de los estados: La triple frontera como 'área gris' en el cono sur americano* [Threats to the Security of States: The Triborder as a 'Grey Area' in the Southern Cone of South America]. Buenos Aires, November 29, 2001. http://www.geocities.com/mcbartolome/triplefrontera1.htm.

Berdal, Mats, and Mónica Serrano, eds. *Transnational Organized Crime & International Security*: *Business as Usual?* Boulder, Colorado: Lynne Rienner, 2002.

Brieger, Pedro, and Enrique Herszkowich. "The Muslim Community of Argentina." *The Muslim World* [Hartford] 92, nos. 1, 2 (Spring 2002): 157–68.

Canadian Security Intelligence Service (CSIS). "Transnational Criminal Activity," November 1998. http://www.fas.org/irp/threat/back10e.htm.

Cliffe, Lionel, and Robin Luckham. "Complex Political Emergencies and the State: Failure and the Fate of the State." *Third World Quarterly* [London] 20, no. 1 (February 1999): 27–50.

Cooke, Melinda Wheeler. "National Security," Chapter 5 in Dennis M. Hanratty and Sandra W. Meditz, eds., *Paraguay: A Country Study*. Washington, DC: Library of Congress, Federal Research Division, 1990, 201–44.

Criminal Intelligence Service Canada (CSIS). "Asian-Based Organized Crime." 1998. http://www.cisc.gc.ca/AnnualReport1998/Cisc1998en/asian98.htm.

Daly, John. "The Suspects: The Latin American Connection," *Jane's Terrorism & Security Monitor* [London], October 1, 2001.

de Morais, Machado, and Andrea Frota. *Money Laundering in Brazil*. Washington, DC: School of Business and Public Management, Institute of Brazilian Business and Management Issues, George Washington University, Fall 2000. http://216.239.51.100/search?q=cache:Ms30X17JQ_YC:www.gwu.edu/~ibi/minerva/Fall 2000/Andrea.Morais.pdf+cc-5+brasil+paraguay&hl=en&ie=UTF-8.

Delpirou, Alain, and Eduardo Mackenzie. *Les cartels criminels: Cocaïne et heroine: Une industrie lourde en Amérique latine*. Paris: Presses Universitaires de France, 2000.

Fayt, Carlos. *Criminalidad del terrorismo sagrado: El atentado a la embajada de Israel en Argentina*. La Plata, Argentina: Editorial Universitaria de La Plata, 2001.

Fields, Jeffrey. Center for Nonproliferation Studies, Monterey Institute of International Studies. "Islamist Terrorist Threat in the Tri-Border Region." October 2002. http://www.nti.org/e_research/e3_16b.html.

Filho, Expedito, and Sílvio Ferreira, with Patrícia Cerqueira. "Rede de clandestinidade" [Clandestine Network], OnlineÉpoca Editora Globo, no. 179 (October 22, 2001).

Finckenauer, James O. "Chinese Transnational Organized Crime: The Fuk Ching" (undated). National Institute of Justice International, U.S. Department of Justice, citing Chin, Ko-lin, *Chinatown Gangs*. Oxford: Oxford University Press, 1996. http://www.ojp.usdoj.gov/nij/international/ctoc.html.

Friedman, Robert I. *Red Mafiya: How the Russian Mob Has Invaded America*. Boston: Little, Brown, 2000.

Goldberg, Jeffrey. "In the Party of God," *The New Yorker* 79, no. 32 (October 28, 2002): 75–83.

Herrera, Eduardo Wills, and Nubia Urueña Corté, with Nick Rosen. "South America." Pages 103–14 in Transparency International, *Global Corruption Report 2003*. Berlin: TI, 2002. http://www.globalcorruptionreport.org/.

Hudson, Rex A. "Narcotics-Funded Terrorist/Extremist Groups in Latin America." Pages 11–39 in Rex A. Hudson, ed., *A Global Overview of Narcotics-Funded Terrorist and Other Extremist Groups*. Washington, DC: Federal Research Division, Library of Congress, May 2002.

Inter-American Development Bank. *Development Beyond Economics: Economic and Social Progress in Latin America - 2000 Report*. Washington, DC: Johns Hopkins University Press and The Inter-American Development Bank, 2000.

International Intellectual Property Alliance. *2003 Special 301 Report: Brazil*, 2003.
    http://www.iipa.com/rbc/2003/2003SPEC301BRAZIL.pdf.

Jordan, David C. *Drug Politics: Dirty Money and Democracies*. Norman, Oklahoma: University
    of Oklahoma Press, 1999.

Junger, Sebastian. "Terrorism's New Geography," *Vanity Fair*, no. 508 (December 2002): 194,
    196, 198–200, 202, 205–6.

Junior, Policarpo. "Tem famosos no meio: Polícia apura um bilionário esquema de remessa
    ilegal de dinheiro ao exterior e já tem nomes de gente graúda" [They Have Famous
    People Among Them: Police Expedite a Billion-Real Scheme for Remitting Illegal
    Money Abroad and Already Have the Names of Big-Shots], *Veja on-line*, no. 1,755 (June
    12, 2002). http://veja.abril.com.br/120602/p_046.html.

Klebnikov, Paul. *Godfather of the Kremlin: Boris Berezovsky and the Looting of Russia*. New
    York: Harcourt Brace, 2000.

Korzeniewicz, Roberto P. "The Society and Its Environment." Chapter 2 in Rex A. Hudson, ed.,
    Argentina: A Country Study. Unpublished manuscript draft. Washington, DC: Library of
    Congress, Federal Research Division, 1999.

Kovadloff, Jacob. *Crisis In Argentina*. American Jewish Community [New York], circa June
    2002. http://www.ajc.org/InTheMedia/PublicationsPrint.asp?did=555.

Kozameh, Ernesto Nicolás, Julio O. Trajtenberg, C.P. Nicolás Kozameh Jr., and Ezequiel
    Trajtenberg. *Guide to the Argentine Executive, Legislative and Judicial System*. July 15,
    2001. http://www.llrx.com/features/argentina.htm.

Madani, Blanca. "Hezbollah's Global Finance Network: The Triple Frontier," *Middle East
    Intelligence Bulletin* [a monthly publication of the United States Committee for a Free
    Lebanon] 4, no. 1 (January 2002).

Madani, Blanca. "New Report Links Syria to 1992 Bombing of Israeli Embassy in Argentina."
    Middle East Intelligence Bulletin 2, no. 3 (March 2000).

Mahan, Sue. *Beyond the Mafia: Organized Crime in the Americas*. Thousand Oaks, CA: Sage,
    1998.

Mendel, William W., "Paraguay's Ciudad del Este and the New Centers of Gravity," *Military
    Review* 82, no. 2 (March–April 2002): 51–58.

Mingardi, Guaracy. "Money and the International Drug Trade in São Paulo," *International
    Social Science Journal*, no. 169 (September 2001): 379–86.

Montoya, Mario Daniel. "Israel Takes Special Interest in Triple Border Area," *Jane's Intelligence Review* [London] 13, no. 12 (December 2001): 13–14.

Montoya, Mario Daniel. "War on Terrorism Reaches Paraguay's Triple Border," *Jane's Intelligence Review* [London] 13, no. 12 (December 2001): 12–15.

Neto, Paulo de Mesquita. *Crime, Violence and Democracy in Latin America.* New Mexico: University of New Mexico, Integration in the Americas Conference, April 5, 2002. http://www.unm.edu/~laiinfo/conference/mesquita.html.

Nurton, James. "Goodbye to a Difficult Year: The World's Leading IP Practices," *Managing Intellectual Property* [London], June 2002, 56–70.

O'Balance, Edgar. *Islamic Fundamentalist Terrorism, 1979-95: The Iranian Connection.* New York: New York University Press, 1997.

Oviedo, Pedro. "En la Triple Frontera se lavan doce mil millones de dólares al año del narcotráfico, según un informe official" [In the Triple Border US$12 Billion Is Laundered Per Year From Narcotics Trafficking, According to An Official Report], www.MisionesOnLine.net, No. 745, July 8, 2001. http://misionesonline.net/paginas/action.lasso?-database=noticias3&-layout=web&-response=noticia.html&id=11349&autorizado=si&-search.

Padilla Fredy, Nelson. "Los hombres de Osama bin Laden en Colombia" [The Men of Osama bin Laden in Colombia], *Cromos*, no. 4,364 (September 24, 2001).

Rauber, Guido. *Lavado de Dinero: Triple Frontera —Work Paper N° 1*, Prevención de Adicciones y Control de Drogas [Subsecretary of Drug Control and Prevention of Addictions], Ministry of Public Health of Misiones Province, Argentina, updated version of December 31, 2000 (original date, August 2, 1999).

Ribeiro Jr., Amaury, and Sonia Filgueiras. "Sieve of Impunity," *Istoé* [Internet Version-www], February 5, 2003, as translated for FBIS, "Brazil: Federal Police, FBI Unveil $30 Billion Money Laundering Scheme," February 5, 2003 (FBIS Document ID: LAP20030203000075).

Richard, Amy O'Neill. "International Trafficking in Women to the United States: A Contemporary Manifestation of Slavery and Organized Crime." An Intelligence Monograph of the Director of Central Intelligence (DCI) Exceptional Intelligence Analyst Program, Center for the Study of Intelligence, Central Intelligence Agency, April 2000, U.S. Department of State, http://usinfo.state.gov/topical/global/traffic/report/homepage.htm#contents (based on interview with INS, New York, May 1999).

Richards, James R. *Transnational Criminal Organizations, Cybercrime, and Money Laundering: A Handbook for Law Enforcement Offices, Auditors, and Financial Investigators.* Boca Raton, Florida: CRC Press LLC, 1999.

Robinson, Jeffrey. *The Laundrymen: Inside Money Laundering, The World's Third-Largest Business*. New York: Arcade, 1996.

Rogers, Bill. "Arabs Accuse Paraguay Police Of Extortion," *Middle East News Online* [Durham, North Carolina], October 4, 2001.

Serrano, Mónica. "Transnational Crime in the Western Hemisphere." Pages 87–112 in Jorge I. Domínguez, ed., *The Future of Inter-American Relations*. An Inter-American Dialogue Book Series. New York and London: Routledge, 2000.

Serrano, Mónica, and María Celia Toro. "From Drug Trafficking to Transnational Organized Crime in Latin America." Chapter 12 in Mats Berdal and Mónica Serrano, eds., *Transnational Organized Crime & International Security: Business as Usual?* Boulder, Colorado: Lynne Rienner, 2002, 155-82.

Silva, Ruy Gomes. *Effective Measures to Combat Transnational Organized Crime in Criminal Justice Processes*. Participants' Papers, 116th International Training Course, Resource Material Series no. 58. Tokyo: Asia and Far East Institute for the Prevention of Crime and the Treatment of Offenders (UNAFEI), December 2001, 160–70. http://www.unafei.or.jp/pdf/58-00.pdf.

Takeyh, Ray, and Nikolas Gvosdev. "Do Terrorist Networks Need a Home?" *Washington Quarterly* 25, no. 3 (2002): 97–108.

Timmerman, Kenneth R. "Likely Mastermind of Tower Attacks: Imad Mugniyeh," *Insight on the News* 17, no. 49 (December 31, 2001): 18–21.

Tollefson, Scott D. "National Security," Chapter 5 in Rex A. Hudson, ed., *Argentina: A Country Study*. Unpublished manuscript draft. Washington, DC: Library of Congress, Federal Research Division, 1999.

United States. Department of State. "Argentina," *Country Reports on Human Rights Practices, 2001*. Washington, DC: Bureau of Democracy, Human Rights, and Labor, March 4, 2002. http://www.state.gov/g/drl/rls/hrrpt/2001/wha/8278.htm.

United States. Department of State. "Brazil," *Country Reports on Human Rights Practices - 2001*. Washington, DC: Bureau of Democracy, Human Rights, and Labor, March 4, 2002.

United States. Department of State. *International Narcotics Control Strategy Report, 1999*. Washington, DC: Bureau for International Narcotics and Law Enforcement Affairs, 2000.

United States. Department of State. *International Narcotics Control Strategy Report, 2002*. Washington, DC: Bureau for International Narcotics and Law Enforcement Affairs, March 1, 2003. http://www.state.gov/g/inl/rls/nrcrpt/2002/html/17952pf.htm.

United States. Department of State. Office of the Coordinator for Counterterrorism. *Patterns of Global Terrorism, 2001*. Washington, DC, May 21, 2002. http://www.state.gov/s/ct/rls/pgtrpt/2001/html/10246.htm.

Webster, William H., Arnaud de Borchgrave, Robert H. Kupperman, Erik R. Peterson, Gerard P. Burke, and Frank J. Cilluffo. *Russian Organized Crime: A Report of the Global Organized Crime Task Force*. CSIS Panel Report Series. Washington, DC: Center for Strategic and International Studies, 1997.

Wilcox, Jr., Philip C. "International Terrorism in Latin America." Testimony to the U.S. House of Representatives, Committee on International Relations, September 28, 1995.

Wills Herrera, Eduardo, and Nubia Urueña Corté, with Nick Rosen. "South America" in Transparency International, *Global Corruption Report 2003*. Berlin: TI, 2002. http://www.globalcorruptionreport.org/.